OECD

MONETARY STUDIES SERIES

THE ROLE OF
MONETARY POLICY
IN
DEMAND MANAGEMENT

THE EXPERIENCE
OF SIX MAJOR COUNTRIES

1975

The Organisation for Economic Co-operation and Development (OECD) was set up under a Convention signed in Paris on 14th December, 1960, which provides that the OECD shall promote policies designed :
- to achieve the highest sustainable economic growth and employment and a rising standard of living in Member countries, while maintaining financial stability, and thus to contribute to the development of the world economy;
- to contribute to sound economic expansion in Member as well as non-member countries in the process of economic development;
- to contribute to the expansion of world trade on a multilateral, non-discriminatory basis in accordance with international obligations.

The Members of OECD are Australia, Austria, Belgium, Canada, Denmark, Finland, France, the Federal Republic of Germany, Greece, Iceland, Ireland, Italy, Japan, Luxembourg, the Netherlands, New Zealand, Norway, Portugal, Spain, Sweden, Switzerland, Turkey, the United Kingdom and the United States.

***

CONTENTS

TABLES

CHARTS

FOREWORD

This report forms part of a series of special studies on monetary policy undertaken by the Secretariat of the OECD at the request of the Economic Policy Committee. Each country has increasingly to formulate its own monetary policies within an international context. The purpose of these studies is to provide a better framework for the analysis of national monetary policies, and for international consultation regarding the use of monetary policy in Member countries for domestic demand management and balance of payments adjustment.

The need for detailed analysis on the working of monetary policy in different countries has been felt for various reasons:

i) In the recent period, increased use has been made of monetary policy, and in more countries than previously, as a means of controlling demand, and as a consequence more evidence is becoming available as to the nature of its impact. It is useful to examine this evidence on an international basis and to compare the effects on demand of monetary policy in different countries.

ii) The volatility of international capital movements and exchange rates has increased. Though the scale of the effects to be attributed to monetary policy is difficult to quantify, the question is clearly of considerable importance for monetary authorities. Since the effects depend on the relative posture of monetary policies in different countries, they can clearly best be evaluated in the context of studies which examine the joint effects of different national monetary policies in at least the major financial centres.

The internal effects of monetary policy depend greatly on the economic and financial structure of the economy including the size of the public debt, the role of banks as financial intermediaries in the saving/investment process, the way in which housing is financed, and the scale and nature of consumer credit. These factors differ much from country to country. The external effects of monetary policy also depend to some extent on general institutional factors peculiar to different countries, and, in some cases, on the use made of policy instruments particularly designed to have external effects.

A series of country studies has, therefore, been carried out which assembles the evidence about the working of monetary policy, taking into account differences in the economic and financial structure and the ways in which they have affected the choice of monetary instruments and the transmission process through which monetary policy has affected the financial and real sectors of the economy. Separate country studies concerning monetary policy in Japan, Italy, Germany, the United States and

5

France have successively been prepared by the Monetary Division of the Department of Economics and Statistics.

The present report represents an attempt to synthesize the results of the individual country studies already finished. In addition, it includes an analysis on the working of monetary policy in the United Kingdom, although a separate, detailed study on this country has not been launched because of the recent important changes in monetary policy management which have made it inopportune to carry it out for the moment. While this study doubtlessly needs to be followed up in the light of further structural changes of the economies, the evolution of monetary management, and progress in the technique of monetary analysis, it nevertheless represents a valuable attempt to integrate various findings on the working of monetary policy in the six major countries.

This general report has been prepared by Kumiharu Shigehara, Head of the Monetary Division of the OECD Secretariat and Niels Thygesen, Professor of Economics at the University of Copenhagen. It was discussed at a meeting of official experts from the six countries, but the views expressed herein are those of the authors, and do not necessarily represent the opinions of the authorities concerned.

September 1974

I

INTRODUCTION

This report aims at analysing the role of monetary policy in short-run demand management in six major OECD countries: France, Germany, Italy, Japan, the United Kingdom and the United States. The study is focused on the period 1960–1972, though reference is made to important developments since 1972. The report is divided into five parts. The present introductory part discusses the general background for monetary policy in the six countries as set out by the main economic trends, the use of fiscal policy and other forms of demand management, and objectives for the use of monetary policy. Part II reviews the main instruments and the design of monetary policy. Part III assesses its impact on financial variables, including domestic monetary aggregates, interest rates and external capital flows. Part IV attempts an assessment of the effects on aggregate demand and its components, while Part V brings out some conclusions of the study.

A. CYCLICAL EXPERIENCES

The six countries covered in the present study differ considerably in their experiences since 1960 with respect to both the average growth rate and its variability. The average growth rate of output in Japan was about twice as high as in France, Germany, Italy and the United States and more than three times as high as in the United Kingdom (Table 1). Yet all six, with the exception of the United States prior to 1965 and Italy after that year, have shared the experience of moving in the "narrow band" as defined by the Heller report,[1] i.e. close to a level of demand that creates inflationary strain in labour and commodity markets.

While quarterly GNP changes reveal the strength of short-run accelerations and decelerations, the growth of real output from year to year has been smooth by historical standards. However, a cyclical pattern has been clearly detectable in at least four of them; Italy and France are in different ways exceptions. To some extent the ability of countries to keep demand growing at a rate approximately equal to potential output[2] was due to automatic stabilizing mechanisms; examples were the tendency for exports to substitute for slack in domestic demand which was observable in the

1. W. Heller and others, *Fiscal Policy for a Balanced Economy*, OECD 1968.
2. For a detailed review of the experience of 18 OECD countries, see "The Measurement of Domestic Cyclical Fluctuations", *OECD Economic Outlook, Occasional Studies*, July 1973.

case of Germany and, to a lesser extent, Japan. In the case of these two countries the operation of this mechanism was much facilitated by a tendency for the cost level of their exportables to rise more slowly than those of their competitors; this tendency gradually became so strong that it was internationally destabilizing and led to adjustments in exchange rates. Changes in fiscal and monetary policy also significantly influenced the course of demand on a number of occasions; a brief review of fiscal policy changes in their cyclical context is found in the following section, while the contribution of monetary policy to the stabilization of internal demand is the major subject of Part IV.

Table 1. FLUCTUATIONS OF DOMESTIC OUTPUT
1960-1972, per cent

	France	Germany	Italy	Japan	UK	US
Average annual growth rate of real GN(D)P....	5.9	4.9	5.2	10.9	3.0	4.0
Standard deviation	0.9	2.5	1.8	3.3	1.2	2.1
Yearly growth rate						
Highest	7.7	8.8	8.3	15.6	5.4	6.6
(year)	(1969)	(1960)	(1961)	(1961)	(1964)	(1966)
Lowest	4.7	-0.2	1.6	4.7	1.3	-0.5
(year)	(1965)	(1967)	(1971)	(1965)	(1962)	(1970)

The main demand components showing cyclical instability were exports and private expenditures. In the *United States*, private capital expenditures (i.e. consumer durables, private fixed investment, and inventory accumulation) accounted for the cycles observed in total demand in the beginning and the end of the 1960s; in both of the two recessions identified by the National Bureau of Economic Research, private capital expenditures declined in real terms. A similar picture is found in the *United Kingdom,* with fixed investment and inventory accumulation as the main causes of cyclical instability; however, a large part of these swings in internal demand were offset in the net foreign balance. Still there were large swings in labour market pressures with a peak in unemployment in early 1963, a low point in 1966 and considerable slack in the economy in 1971-72. In *Japan*, demand pressures have been generated by booms in inventories and non-residential fixed investment; in recent phases there was a strong offset in the foreign balance. *Germany* presents a somewhat different picture in that exports appear to have generated the three strong booms observed in 1959-1960, 1963 and 1968-69; the rise in exports subsequently triggered an upturn first in private investment, then in consumption.

The two remaining countries, France and Italy, appear in some respects to be exceptions to the above conclusions. *France* has had the smoothest growth of demand of the six countries, and a significant gap between actual and potential output has hardly opened up at any time. In *Italy,* instability has been caused both by investment and consumption (inventory accumulation cannot be separated from consumption in Italian national accounts); sharp upward adjustments of wages and salaries in 1963 and 1969 tended to generate the only two short phases of strong demand pressure observed.

8

The foreign balance remained strong as a nearly permanent source of net demand from 1964 onwards, but slack in the domestic economy persisted; the Italian experiences since about the mid-1960s can hardly be classified as cyclical problems.

In most countries the main source of cyclical instability has accordingly been observed in private investment and the demand for consumer durables. These expenditures are to a considerable extent financed by borrowing. *A priori,* it would appear that monetary policy has natural advantages as a tool of economic stabilization; by varying interest rates and flows of credit at an early enough stage, the authorities could apparently achieve the smoothing of total demand desired. This optimistic conclusion is often thought to be unwarranted for two main reasons. First, the time lag in policy effects may be so long as to place unrealistic demands on the ability of the authorities to forecast the course of expenditures; the effects of varying monetary instruments may take so long to build up that the authorities destabilize the economy further by vigorous use of them. This is a major contention of some leading monetarists who advocate the policy of steady monetary expansion over time rather than discretionary actions. Though some of the evidence reviewed in the *OECD Monetary Studies Series* on which the present comparative analysis relies supports the conclusion that the effects of monetary policy build up over time, the short run effects seem on the whole strong enough to leave an important role for discretionary policy. Secondly, it may be technically easier (or more effective in regulating total demand) to change other, notably fiscal, instruments. There is little evidence, however, to suggest that this is the case. On balance, therefore, monetary policy clearly retains an important short-term role.

In recent years the emphasis in policy design has shifted somewhat away from smoothing fluctuations in real demand towards the dampening of inflation. This shift is inadequately represented in the present study which focuses on experiences in the 1960s and the very early 1970s. Nevertheless, the evidence presented is relevant also in a situation where the policy-makers seem preoccupied more permanently with anti-inflationary measures. Particular attention is given in this study to periods of monetary restraint when the combination of actions deployed has not been very different from those that form the main part of the anti-inflationary policies of recent years. Furthermore, some evidence is presented on the association of price accelerations and decelerations to changes in the stance of monetary policy, though this association is obviously indirect and subject to considerable uncertainty; it is also likely to shift over time as inflationary expectations spread through financial and commodity markets.

B. FISCAL POLICY AND OTHER FORMS OF DEMAND MANAGEMENT

The experiences of the six countries are not easily summarized, and the problem of measurement of the fiscal impact remains serious. While the simplest procedure is to use public expenditure or the measured budget surplus, it is preferable as a measure of the actions of the authorities to use a figure which excludes the automatic response of public finances. One such summary measure is the concept of " high employment surplus " developed in the United States. It measures the difference between a hypothetical revenue figure, viz. government revenues corresponding to a high level of resource utilization, and actual government expenditures (corrected

9

for any departure of actual unemployment benefits from those corresponding to high employment). While the high employment surplus conceals important information by not allowing for the differential impact on GNP of different categories of expenditures and revenues, changes in the surplus provide the most convenient single measure of the fiscal thrust. For this reason similar measures for the other countries, except the United Kingdom, have been brought together in Charts 1 to 4 and 6. The fiscal indicator used in Chart 5 for the United Kingdom is calculated from the recorded totals of revenues and expenditures and is therefore influenced by fluctuations of economic activity.[1]

An evaluation of the selected fiscal indicators suggests two broad conclusions:

 i) changes in fiscal impulse have been a major influence on the course of GNP; and
 ii) they have far from always been in the anticyclical direction required by stabilization policy, though there are clear improvements from the first to the second half of the 13-year period surveyed.

The magnitude of the thrust was particularly large and sustained in the cases of the United States and the United Kingdom. In the former, the high employment budget moved fairly steadily from a surplus of about 6 per cent of GNP in 1960 to a deficit of 2 per cent in 1967-68; this was clearly a major cause behind the unprecedented long upswing which initially absorbed the idle resources and subsequently created inflationary strain. There was then a sharp reversal between early 1968 and late 1969, corresponding to a direct cumulative impact of nearly 4 per cent; from late 1969 there was again a large fiscal stimulus. In the United Kingdom there was a major gradual tightening of fiscal policy (taxation) between 1967 and 1970, and a stimulus of the same magnitude from late 1970 onwards. The experience of the other four countries is less marked by such long swings in fiscal impulses, though it may be noted that Germany went through a prolonged easing in the 1963-66 period which was reversed in 1968-69, and that Italy has been pursuing generally expansionary policies in recent years.

The stabilizing role of fiscal policy cannot be assessed adequately by means of the set of indicators here available; for one thing, such an assessment would require information on the likely time lags involved in magnifying through a multiplier process the direct fiscal impact suggested by the indicator. Nevertheless, it is possible to conclude from the evidence as well as from information on changes in the institutional framework that the counter-cyclical role of fiscal policy has been strengthened in recent years. In Japan, the constraint of budgetary balance was abandoned from 1965; fiscal policy has since played a much more active role, notably in an expansionary direction in 1971-72. In Germany, the legislation on stability and growth enacted in 1967 made possible more prompt adjustments of public expenditure, and revenue changes have been brought into use on several occasions. Despite these and other steps in the direction of more flexible use of policy instruments, it remains true that the lags involved in deciding upon fiscal policy changes are long. Monetary policy has therefore inevitably been called upon to perform major tasks of internal stabilization — subject to the constraints imposed by the need to preserve a high degree of stability in foreign exchange and domestic financial markets.

1. The sources of these series and the degree of OECD Secretariat estimation involved are reported in the notes to the charts. For the U.K., Italy and Japan only annual estimates are available; for the other three countries the series are quarterly.

In recent years, fiscal and monetary policy have to an increasing extent been supplemented by other instruments, designed to dampen the general tendency for prices to accelerate and balance of payments developments to get out of hand. Direct intervention into prices and incomes has occurred on a large scale in the United States since 1971 and in the United Kingdom since 1972; in the latter country, a number of experiments with incomes policy were made in the course of the 1960s. In the recent inflationary upswing other countries, too, have found traditional approaches to restraint inadequate; most of the six countries are presently, in one form or another, intervening directly in the formation of selected prices and incomes. It is not possible to regard the use of such instruments as substitutes for traditional short-term changes in fiscal and monetary policy; incomes policies have been designed primarily to achieve a degree of competitiveness in domestic and foreign markets. They have been viewed as a socially less disruptive alternative to the correction of a fundamental disequilibrium in the external account through a devaluation. In practice, the two types of policies – the intervention into prices and incomes and substantial devaluations – have accompanied and supplemented each other in the two Anglo-Saxon countries faced with large external deficits, but in neither of the two cases have they relieved monetary policy of its tasks in short-run demand management. Once more, in the recent upswing, monetary policy has filled its traditional role as a major instrument of short-run stabilization.[1]

The introduction of comprehensive measures to restrain prices and incomes and the substantial changes in parities (or central rates) which have occurred since the devaluation of sterling in November 1967 have not modified the tasks confronting monetary policy and other instruments of stabilization policy or the way in which these policies work. However, the widening of the permissible band around parities or central rates from December 1971 and the subsequent widespread floating in 1972–73 are developments capable of changing the scope and *modus operandi* of monetary policy. These new factors are referred to only very briefly in the main part of the present report, which aims at summarizing the experiences of the six countries up to 1972 as they emerged from the individual country studies.

C. OBJECTIVES OF MONETARY POLICY

Charts 1–6 present selected indicators of demand pressure and policy changes. The main domestic indicator of demand pressure is the GNP gap, i.e. the percentage by which actual demand falls short of (or exceeds) calculated capacity.[2] This measure of slack is supplemented by the unemployment series most frequently used to assess pressures in the labour market in that particular country. In some cases this is an unemployment percentage, and in others it is the relation between offers and vacancies in the labour market. It is not suggested that these precise series were actually the ones watched by the authorities. In some cases they could not have been, since they have been constructed subsequently with the

---

1. See, e.g. *OECD Economic Outlook*, December 1973.
2. For a discussion of the GNP gap calculations, see "The Measurement of Domestic Cyclical Fluctuations", *OECD Economic Outlook, Occasional Studies*, July 1973.

benefit of hindsight. Nevertheless they provide a useful starting point for assessing in which situations monetary policy was called upon to either restrain demand or expand it. Periods in which monetary policy was used to restrain demand are shaded in the charts. For the United Kingdom, they generally represent periods starting from the time of the first announced actions of monetary restraint and ending at that of monetary relaxation. The detailed justification for the dating of the phases of restrictive policy in the other countries will be found in the Secretariat's five national monetary studies.

In addition to the GNP gap and unemployment indicator, the charts show two other measures of major policy objectives, namely the rate of change of prices and an indicator of external imbalance. The nature of the relevant price index may vary from country to country; in all cases both consumer and wholesale price indices are shown. In most countries political interest appears to focus on consumer prices; Japan may be an exception in that wholesale prices have figured prominently in the public discussion. Major phases of restraint, as indicated by the shaded areas, have invariably been introduced at times of pressure on domestic resources indicated by a relatively low unemployment percentage and a rate of growth of prices, fast by historical standards and usually accelerating. The evaluation of what constitutes a dangerous level of pressure appears to have been modified since 1960. For example, in Japan pressure on the labour market was higher just prior to the introduction of the third and fourth phases of restraint than at the start of the two earlier ones. In the United States monetary expansion was allowed to get underway in 1970 while unemployment was lower than was the case at the start of the 1960-62 expansionary phase; and the rate of change of prices was far higher in 1970. There is apparently a process of "getting used to pressure" and possibly a firmer political commitment to the minimization of unemployment towards the end of the period. However, conclusions in this area are necessarily hazardous, because it is hardly possible to disentangle, in the observed use of monetary policy, on the one hand possible shifts in the relative importance of various aims of policy − the prevailing political view of the trade-off between price stability and employment − and on the other hand changes in the anticipated efficiency of monetary policy. Using again the two expansionary phases of United States monetary policy as an illustration, the switch to expansion at the beginning of 1970 may also have been prompted by a negative evaluation of the efficiency with which the preceding period of monetary restraint had affected inflationary pressures.

Two measures of external imbalance are presented in Charts 1-6: the balance on current account and the change in official reserves, both measured in per cent of GNP. Because of the conceptual difficulties involved in measuring the international liquidity of the two key currency countries, only the former indicator is shown for the United States and the United Kingdom. There are two aspects of particular interest in the observed movements in these indicators; their relative size and their degree of synchronization with indicators of domestic imbalance. The former conveys a relevant impression of the magnitude of the offsetting actions required; the latter points to the emergence of so-called dilemma situations in which external and internal considerations pull in opposite directions.

Looking at the relative size of imbalances, the amplitude of the current account series appears to have been rather stable throughout the 1960s. The maximum imbalance observed is that of Italy which moved in the 3-4 per cent range during 1965-69. For the other five countries the surplus or deficit never exceeded 2 per cent in any one year; in the United States it never reached 1 per cent of GNP. The only two countries for which there is a clearly discernible trend in the imbalance throughout the 1960-1972 period are the United States, where the current surplus was shrinking at an accelerating rate from the mid-1960s until the emergence of a substantial deficit in 1972, and Japan which saw its balance strengthen from a modest deficit in most years prior to 1965 to a sizeable surplus in 1971-72. The U.K. current balance improved very considerable during 1969-1971, but then suffered a sharp reversal in 1972.

Though the level of a country's current account imbalance will be a relevant consideration in the design of policy, recently observed or projected changes in that imbalance may be even more important. A worsening of the current account might well lead to a reconsideration of policy, even when the starting position is one of surplus; on the contrary, a strengthening of the current account is typically considered a sign that demand management policies are successful and should be continued rather than as a justification for revising them. There is some crude evidence as reported in Charts 1-6 on such asymmetries between reactions to upward and downward changes in the current balance and, more generally, on the weight which individual countries attach to movements in their current balance relative to movements in purely domestic indicators.

In a typical case, indicators of domestic pressure — the GNP gap and labour market pressure series and relevant price indices — move in the same direction as the current account. An upturn in domestic demand reduces slack, increases the upward pressure on prices, generates higher import flows and may also divert resources from export industries into production for the home market. The size of the marginal propensity to import and the ease with which resources may be switched from internal to external uses are the main determinants of the degree of synchronization. To the extent that these movements are nearly parallel, the signs of overheating will appear concurrently in the internal and external indicators, and it will be possible to determine what caused a tightening of policy — and its subsequent relaxation — only after a careful interpretation of events. Such a concurrence of internal and external indicators may be observed, for example, in the cases of Italy, Japan and the United Kingdom. Thus the introduction of monetary restraint in Italy in 1963 and 1969 was preceded by a sharp deterioration in the current account following an acceleration of domestic prices and costs, and its subsequent relaxation by a clear recovery in the current account and some abatement of inflationary pressures. Japan was another example until the late 1960s; in the three early phases of restraint it was a major objective of policy to improve the current account, and a substantial strengthening was the main motive for the removal of restraint in the three cases about one year later. But movements in the current account tended to be closely synchronized with those in indicators of domestic pressure.[1] In the United Kingdom the protection of the current account was even more dominant among policy objectives due to the exposed position of sterling. While the U.K. current account tended to move parallel to domestic indicators, its sensitivity to changes in internal pressures appeared so considerable as to put external considerations into the foreground (page 14).

The German economy — and the Japanese economy after the 1967-68 restrictive phase — represent exceptions to this general situation. In Germany

1. OECD Monetary Studies Series, *Monetary Policy in Japan*, pp. 58-62.

the main generating force of boom conditions has been spurts in exports. Three strong export booms in 1959–1960, 1963 and 1968–69 triggered an upsurge in domestic demand, mainly business fixed investment; with a somewhat longer lag, private consumption expenditure rose at a rate well above its long-run trend.[1] This cyclical pattern of demand implied that a worsening of the current account set in only rather late in the economic upswing as the induced additional imports caught up with the increase in exports. Monetary restraint was introduced in all three cases in a situation of current surplus, before any significant deterioration had set in; and a deterioration got underway only during the restrictive phases. When restraint was lifted in the first and third phases – late 1960 and late 1971 respectively – the current account position was actually worse than at the introduction of restraint. The 1969–1970 restrictive phase in Japan represents a similar situation ; restraint was introduced at a time when a boom in Japan's exports had pulled the current account into large surplus, and it was lifted at a time when the surplus had changed only little. It would seem legitimate to regard at least the 1959–1960 and 1969–1971 restrictive phases in Germany and the 1969–1970 restrictive phase in Japan as illustrations of dilemma situations in which the internal and external indicators give conflicting signs. Since the imposition and lifting of restrictive monetary measures both appear to have been largely unrelated to movements in the current account, it may be concluded that the dilemma was resolved by putting the emphasis on internal indicators, at least in initiating restraint.

The experiences of Germany, and more recently Japan, are examples of a combination of a current balance surplus and a domestic economy in high gear – a situation indicative of fundamental external disequilibrium and as such justifying an adjustment of exchange rates. An example of an opposite dilemma situation in which the current account is weak even when the domestic economy is well below full utilization of resources is provided by the experience of the United Kingdom at times during the 1960s and that of the United States in the early 1960s. The two countries chose different solutions to their dilemmas; the United Kingdom persisted in tight monetary policies throughout most of the second half of the 1960s at a time when GNP was below potential. It was only when, reinforced by the 1967 devaluation and tight fiscal policies for three consecutive years thereafter, the current balance had swung back into surplus and remained there for some time that a significant change in the stance of monetary policy was made. In the United States, on the other hand, monetary expansion was maintained through 1960–62 to reduce unemployment despite a historically weak current account. It was gradually phased out, not because of external considerations, but because fiscal policy was assuming a more active role. The difference in reaction in the two countries was primarily a result of the greater urgency of the objective of improving the current account in the United Kingdom. When the United States entered a second phase of expansionary monetary policy in 1970 at a time when the current account was much weaker than in 1960–62, it proved necessary to introduce wide-ranging supplementary measures to deal with the mounting external imbalance.

External objectives have concerned not only current balances but also changes in international liquidity, i.e. the sum of the current account and net capital flows (public and private, bank and non-bank, flows). Such changes are relevant in the assessment of the outlook for exchange rate

1. OECD Monetary Studies Series, *Monetary Policy in Germany*, pp. 9-13.

stability and for freedom of action in demand management, and most countries therefore have had at various times vaguely formulated aims with respect to their international liquidity and its permissible rate of change. The basic assumption about an international economic system in which exchange rate flexibility is narrowly circumscribed, such as that prevailing prior to the summer of 1971, is that private capital flows will tend to be stabilizing. According to such an assumption, if the authorities were to do nothing to sterilize, say, a current account deficit, the tendency for velocity and interest rates to rise would induce net capital inflows, the elasticity depending amongst other things on the degree of capital restrictions maintained by that country. There might also be some automatic inflow in the form of trade credit linked to the faster growth of imports than of exports. Movements in an outward direction would be generated by a current account surplus. If these forces were operative — and it would be in the power of the authorities to reinforce them by strongly counter-cyclical domestic policies and supplement them by public borrowing and lending abroad — one would expect the observed changes in international liquidity to be different from and generally smaller than the current account imbalances. There is, however, little in the experiences of the four countries here surveyed — the two reserve currency countries are left aside because of the difficulties involved in measuring changes in their international liquidity — which confirms this theory, at least as an automatic response.

In *Japan,* changes in international liquidity mirrored current account imbalances during the early 1960s.[1] Subsequently reserves remained nearly constant; this was mainly the result of changes in foreign exchange regulations and the authorities' special operations in borrowing and lending. The working of the classical adjustment mechanism probably played only a secondary role. During the period of very large surpluses in 1971 there were large-scale net inflows of capital on top of the current account surplus; but, during the subsequent period of continuing surpluses, the authorities succeeded in stabilizing Japan's international liquidity through a variety of measures.

Italy appears to fit the classical adjustment mechanism more closely; despite the sizeable current surpluses in every year between 1964 and 1972, Italy's international liquidity increased only moderately, reflecting an outflow of private non-bank funds. At times, particularly in 1969 but also in 1972, the outflow went beyond what could be considered desirable and induced a tightening of policy at a time when both the current surplus and the existence of unused domestic resources seemed to permit monetary expansion and low interest rates. In 1973 the Italian authorities basically modified the background to monetary policy through a series of measures comprising devaluation through floating, a two-tier exchange market and capital controls. It is too early to judge whether this has basically modified past patterns of action by the monetary authorities in which the introduction (and removal) of restraint was largely dictated by changes in Italy's international liquidity.

In the case of *Germany* the amplitude of changes in international liquidity has been wider than that of current account imbalances. This emerges with particular clarity during the restrictive phases in 1960 and 1970. As indicated on page 14 above, the current account was in surplus throughout the 1959–1960 and the 1969–1971 restrictive phases, since the booms which restraint was designed to cool off had originally been trig-

---

1. OECD Monetary Studies Series, *Monetary Policy in Japan*, pp. 38 ff.

gered by a strong rise in exports. It is therefore clear that the introduction of restraint was motivated by internal considerations. But the lifting of restraint in late 1960 and its modification in mid-1970 were not so motivated; they were caused by the tendency for capital inflows to swell Germany's international liquidity at a faster rate than acceptable. These experiences with the inability of the authorities to keep the degree of monetary stringency required for internal purposes provided a powerful motive for modifying the background for policy through revaluation, floating and some degree of capital controls. Experiences in 1972–73 suggest that the modified regime has not fully eliminated the powerful interaction of current surpluses and capital inflows. These flows were generated partly by relatively tighter domestic monetary conditions and partly also by expectations of revaluation.

Changes in *France's* international liquidity have in recent years come to be dominated to an increasing extent by transactions other than those related to the current account, the latter having been relatively close to equilibrium. Heavy capital outflows in 1968 on top of a widening current account deficit prompted the introduction of restraint late in that year; and the reversal of these trends, facilitated by the intervening devaluation of the franc, was a major factor behind the lifting of restraint in 1970. Subsequently capital restrictions were intensified and a two-tier foreign exchange market established; and the gradual tightening of monetary policy in 1973 represents a test — the outcome of which must still await judgement — of the extent to which policy measures designed for internal considerations can be effective.

In summary, it may be concluded that conflicting signs on the one hand from indicators of internal pressure, notably unemployment and price statistics, and on the other hand from the current account have been relatively rare. They have either been short-term dilemmas due to a prominent role for exports in the earlier phases of an upswing (Germany's export booms prior to the late 1960s) or longer-term ones pointing to a fundamental external disequilibrium (Japan and Germany prior to the currency realignments of 1971 and the United Kingdom prior to the 1967 devaluation). In these latter cases, the conflict has tended to be resolved in an asymmetrical way, the surplus countries putting the main emphasis on internal stability in designing restrictive measures and the deficit country finding itself constrained to aim primarily for a greater degree of external balance.

When one looks at the removal of restraint and the external constraints imposed by mobile capital, the asymmetry between surplus and deficit countries tends to disappear. In the absence of tight capital controls, the inability of Germany to pursue monetary restraint seemed as pronounced as the inability the United Kingdom would have faced if it had attempted expansionary monetary policies at the time when sterling was generally thought to be overvalued. An external constraint in the form of limits to what is considered an acceptable rate of change of a country's international liquidity is a feature shared by surplus and deficit countries in a regime of relatively rigid exchange rates. The wider the limits of tolerance within which international liquidity is allowed to fluctuate, the less the constraint matters, and countries have, with increasing inventiveness, attempted to dampen the volatility of their reserves by imposing more comprehensive capital controls. Yet there is little doubt that the degree of financial integration has increased to such an extent during the years since 1960 that

16

the usual assumption of stabilizing capital flows to offset current account imbalances has often been misleading. Flows have at times overcompensated such imbalances, at other times accentuated them, depending on the importance of changes in relative monetary conditions and of speculation in exchange rate adjustments. These experiences will be reviewed in Part III.

Chart 1. SELECTED INDICATORS OF DEMAND PRESSURE AND ECONOMIC POLICY
FRANCE

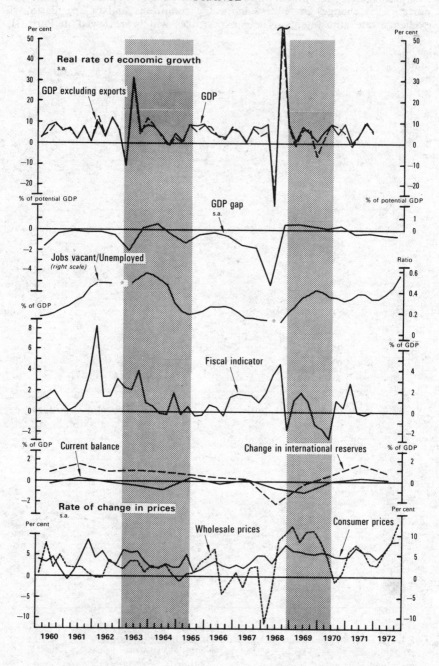

* Strikes

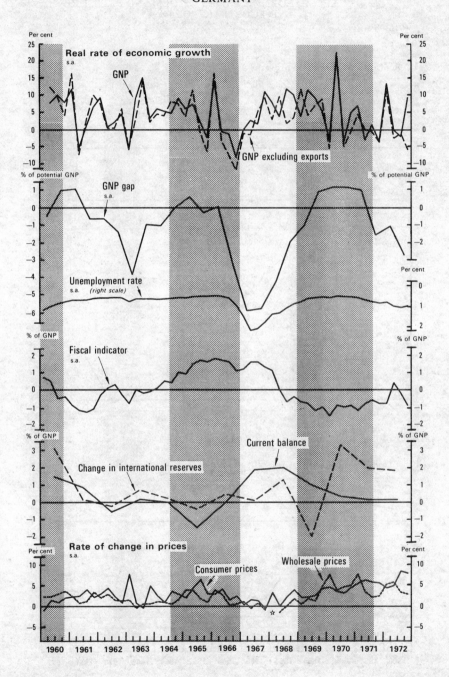

*   Strikes

Chart 3. SELECTED INDICATORS OF DEMAND PRESSURE AND ECONOMIC POLICY
ITALY

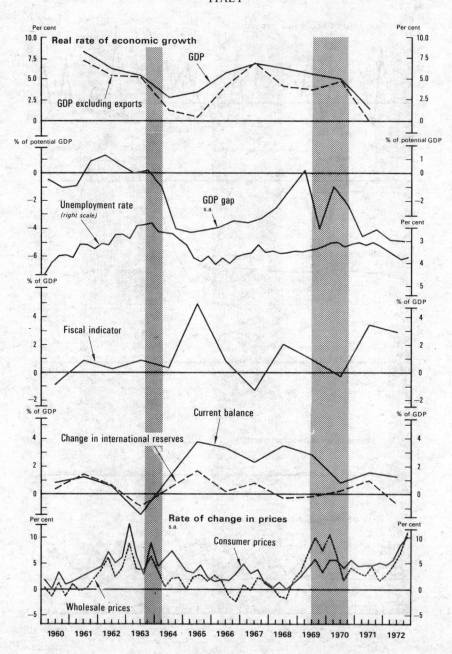

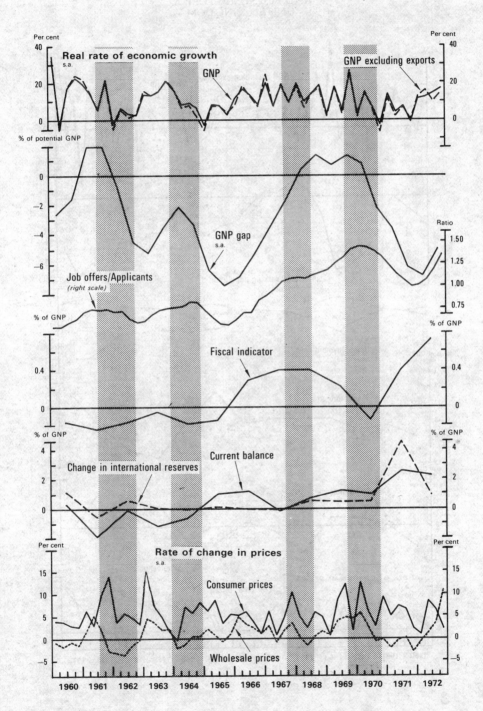

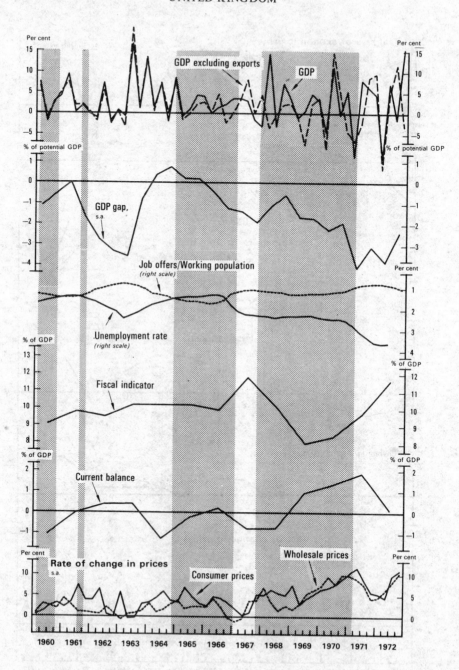

Chart 6. SELECTED INDICATORS OF DEMAND PRESSURE
AND ECONOMIC POLICY
UNITED STATES

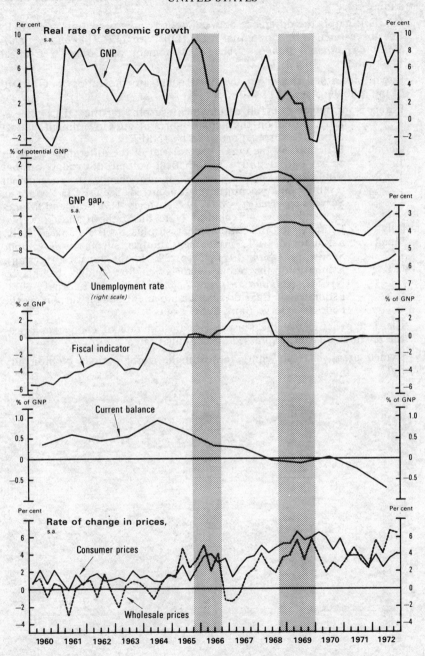

1. The first panel shows the seasonally adjusted rate of growth of real GN(D)P over the previous quarter (year for Italy), expressed at an annual rate.

2. GN(D)P gap is the difference between actual and "potential" GN(D)P. For the estimates of "potential" GN(D)P, see *OECD Economic Outlook, Occasional Studies.* "The Measurement of Domestic Cyclical Fluctuations", July 1973.

3. Fiscal indicators shown in the third panel are the ratios to GN(D)P of the following series.

France : Estimates of full employment surplus by the OECD Secretariat based on the actual figures of the Government budget deficit (or surplus) provided by INSEE.

Germany: Estimates by the OECD Secretariat of the differences between actual output and a hypothetical volume of production that would have been achieved if no change in government revenue and expenditure had occurred. See OECD Economic Surveys, *Germany,* May 1973, Annex I: Fiscal and Monetary Indicators – Technical Note on Methods and Concepts.

Italy : Estimates of full employment surplus by the Bank of Italy.

Japan: Estimates of full employment budget surplus in *Economic Survey of Japan,* 1971–72 (p. 290 in the Japanese version).

U.K. : Estimates of the public sector's weighted budget balance by NIESR. *National Institute Economic Review,* February 1973.

U.S.: Estimates of quarterly full employment budget surplus by the Federal Reserve Bank of St. Louis.

4. The last panel shows the seasonally adjusted rate of change in prices over the previous quarter, expressed at an annual rate.

5. Shaded areas in each chart represent the major periods of monetary restraint.

II

MONETARY INSTRUMENTS
AND THE DESIGN OF MONETARY POLICY

A. A SURVEY OF INSTRUMENT USE

Monetary policy in six countries so diverse in their financial structure and their cyclical experiences is bound to be conducted in different ways. Indeed, the following survey will bring out that, historically, the instruments relied on have differed very widely, between the dominant use of open market operations in the United States at one end and, at the other, the importance of ceilings on bank credit and other financial flows in Japan, France and until recently also in the United Kingdom. However, the use of policy instruments is evolving constantly in the light of the experience gained, and there is always the danger of misinterpreting a temporary relaxation of policy as a more basic modification in the use of instruments. The experiences of the last few years supply a clear example of this. During the slack in activity which developed in a number of countries from 1970 onwards, monetary policy was generally relaxed; credit ceilings were dropped in the United Kingdom and France and there appeared, in general, to be a movement away from direct methods of control and towards reliance on more flexible instruments, notably open market operations and frequent discount rate changes. But the very strong boom in most economies in 1972–73 pushed the monetary authorities back into a very restrictive stance where recourse to the widest possible range of instruments seemed desirable. A convergence of methods of monetary management emerges as the principal conclusion that can be drawn at the present time.

There are several examples to support this conclusion. The development of a comprehensive set of instruments to deal with inflows and outflows of private non-bank funds — movements of bank funds were already regulated in most cases — has been an important feature in five of the six countries; the United States has remained an exception. The more active use of changes in central bank lending rates and of transactions in securities markets are additional examples. The aim of obtaining a better grip on bank lending has led to:

    i) the introduction of ceilings for major categories of bank loans in Italy;

    ii) the reintroduction of quantitative controls on bank credit in Japan;

    iii) the introduction of credit guidelines and highly punitive reserve requirements against increases in bank lending above the norm in France;

iv) the introduction of supplementary reserve requirements against increases in the main financial institutions' interest-bearing liabilities (the main counterpart of credit) above a certain level in the United Kingdom; and

v) the consideration of a proposal to obtain the authority for imposing credit ceilings and reserve requirements against credit in new legislation in Germany; there has been discussion of a similar step in the United States though it seems unlikely that ceilings would be feasible given the very large number of banks there.

The monetary authorities are often faced with a dilemma between the long-run aim of smoothly operating financial markets and the need to achieve a significant restraining effect on private demand in the short run. Some measures such as ceilings on various types of financial flows are undoubtedly effective in the latter sense, but they may have harmful implications for the long-run aim if they are kept in existence beyond a short period. It is therefore not surprising that monetary policy at times gives the impression of constant experimentation and even vacillation when the need for a major change in policy stance arises. Another example of such apparent hesitation on the strategic approach to monetary policy may be found in the attitude to interest rates in depository institutions. Although there has been in recent years the general tendency towards the weakening of institutional arrangements in the banking sector which ensured the authorities' firm influence on bank lending and deposit rates, the practical effect of abolishing such arrangements does not seem to have been very great (pages 45-47).

The remainder of the present section will summarize the position with respect to the use of major instruments of monetary policy: purchases and sales of securities, changes in the availability and cost of central bank lending, changes in reserve requirement ratios, direct ceilings on bank lending and other forms of credit flows, administrative control over interest rates and control over foreign transactions of banks and non-banks. In the case of each of these instruments the review is introduced by comments on their comparative advantages; the past practices of individual countries are then summarized, the order of countries being suggested by the relative importance they appear to have given to the particular instrument. The design of instrument use, i.e. the operating strategy in which countries have typically combined the possible courses of action open to them, is taken up in section B of the present part.

a) *Purchase and sale of securities*

The purchase and sale of securities by the central bank is an instrument available in all six countries. The main advantage of this instrument is its flexibility; operations can be undertaken in arbitrarily small amounts and at the discretion of the central banks. Two major considerations arise in the design of the transactions: whether they should be confined to government securities, which is normally the case, and to short-term instruments; and whether they should be undertaken solely with banks or also with the non-bank public. It is obviously a prerequisite for effective use of the instrument that a well-developed securities market exists. If this is not the case, it will often be an important aim of the central bank to help bring such a market into existence.

The scope for central bank transactions in securities is accordingly closely linked with the structure and management of the public debt. The need to facilitate the financing of public debt has sometimes forced the

26

hand of the central bank, in the sense that the long-term aim of securing a steady market had to take precedence over the short-term aim of influencing the money supply or interest rates in some "appropriate" counter-cyclical way. It is not suggested that there is always or even normally a clear conflict between the two types of aims, but only that adherence to stability in the bond market will limit the capacity of open market operations to achieve stability in a broader sense, viz. in commodity and labour markets. The clearest examples of the predominance of long-term aims were the important stabilizing role of the central banks of Italy and the United Kingdom in their respective markets for government bonds prior to 1969 and 1971, respectively. In France, Germany and Japan, the scope for genuine open market operations has long been limited either by the authorities' preference to deal only with the banks or by the structure of securities markets which have not been sufficiently widely based to make substantial transactions with the non-bank public possible. Central bank transactions in securities markets have therefore had more limited technical objectives, though the situation may be evolving fast in this respect in the three countries; see page 28. The following paragraphs will summarize the main features of the use of this policy instrument in individual countries.

In the *United States,* the purchase and sale of securities in the open market is the dominant instrument both for offsetting short-term fluctuations and for effecting major changes in bank reserves. The monthly meetings of the main policy-making body, the Federal Open Market Committee (FOMC), focus on formulating general instructions to be given to the Open Market Manager who conducts such transactions.[1] Among various types of transactions, operations in which the original purchase (or sale) is reversed within a short period often dominate; these so-called "repurchase agreements" are particularly useful for offsetting short-run fluctuations in other sources of reserve money. Transactions take place primarily in government securities; they are concentrated at the short end of the market. Long-term securities have been purchased at times, but no outright sales have been undertaken since the market is not thought to have the breadth and resilience necessary to sustain large-scale interventions. The Federal Reserve has always wanted not to be seen to assume direct responsibility for long-term interest rates. Trading takes place through dealers with both banks and non-banks; the active participation of a large number of transactors in the money market assures that Federal Reserve operations are quickly and widely felt in financial markets. Operations are co-ordinated with Treasury debt management; but it appears that there are no major constraints on the use of open market operations except possibly in the short intervals (known as "even-keel" periods) between the announcement and the marketing of large issues of Treasury debt.

In the *United Kingdom,* open market operations have also been very important, but their purpose was rather different.[2] The Bank of England

1. A detailed review of the role of open market operations and the evolution of the strategy of the FOMC in designing it may be found in OECD Monetary Studies Series, *Monetary Policy in the United States*, Part II and Appendix II.
2. The **Bank's** aims were at one point (1966) expressed in the following way: "The need to refinance maturing debt together with the need to borrow to finance new capital investment and the certain prospects for many years to come that these pressing needs will both persist, enable the chief purpose of debt management to be stated simply: it is to maintain market conditions that will maximize, both now and in the future, the desire of investors at home and abroad to hold British government debt". *The Bank of England Quarterly Bulletin*, June 1966.

sees itself primarily as the government's banker with the responsibility of creating a large and expanding market in long-term government debt; in this way the creation of highly liquid assets such as Treasury bills as a result of the large borrowing requirements of the government is minimized. This strategy does not typically require the Bank of England to take the initiative in dealing, but rather to respond to sales offers and bids in the market for government securities. The Bank's active choice lies in the prices at which it is ready to make transactions and in the advice it gives to the Treasury on how public debt issues should be tailored to meet the demand by large investors. Since the reform of monetary policy introduced in 1971 (see page 42), the Bank has established that it is not obliged to conduct outright support operations in the market for longer maturities, i.e., more than one year; this modification of policy has not so far led to markedly greater movements in interest rates. While dealings at the long end of the market cover a wider range of transactors, the market for Treasury bills is largely confined to discount houses, private banks and foreign official institutions. The Bank has in recent years begun to intervene in other short-term financial markets, notably the market for local authority deposits. As the Treasury bill market has declined in relative importance — partly due to the success of the monetary authorities in limiting the recourse to short-term financing — these other markets have tended to provide better indications of short-term financial pressures.

In *Italy,* the role of open market operations has in several respects been similar to that in the United Kingdom. The securities market is large and active; it is dominated by government bonds widely held by financial institutions, individuals and corporations, meeting the preconditions for an active policy of open market operations. However, since the very substantial government deficits required to provide an expansionary thrust in an economy with widespread under-utilization of resources caused the supply of bonds to outgrow demand, the Bank of Italy adopted from 1966 a policy of stabilizing the bond rate by declaring its readiness to undertake operations at a fixed rate.[1] This policy of pegging rates was continued until 1969, but the active involvement of the Bank did not lead to any massive increase in its portfolio, since the stability of rates appeared to induce a significant upward shift in the demand for bonds by the private sector. In fact, it was only after the abandonment of pegging in 1969 that the Bank undertook substantial support operations mainly in the form of subscriptions to Treasury debt prior to issue; but long-term rates have been allowed to vary substantially in recent years. Since short-term financial markets are not highly developed, Bank of Italy transactions have been concentrated in long-term securities.

While transactions in securities have been an important policy instrument for effecting changes in reserve money and interest rates in the three countries reviewed above, they have tended to play a more modest role in the three other countries under study. In France, Germany and Japan, the emphasis has been heavily on security transactions with the private banks. Mostly, the transactions have been of a form which makes them difficult to distinguish from temporary central bank lending through discounting or advances against collateral. *France* has offered the clearest example of such a policy with a reliance on day-to-day transactions with the banks to provide a convenient way for the banks to even out very

---

1. OECD Monetary Studies Series, *Monetary Policy in Italy*, pp. 22 and 77-78.

short-term fluctuations in reserve positions. Since 1971, interventions by the Bank of France in the inter-bank money market have developed into the main continuous source of central bank credit to the banking system. In June 1973 new outright purchase operations in private discountable bills and some other instruments were introduced. Banks are expected to submit at certain intervals their requests for additional reserves — "*appel d'offres*" — but these requests may be met only in part. The similarity with open market operations is therefore less than complete.[1] In *Germany* transactions have also in the past been largely confined to banks and to money market instruments, but they have recently been enlarged in both respects, as the non-banking sector has been encouraged to participate more actively in securities markets at both the short and long ends. In *Japan,* transactions have gradually developed beyond the bilateral outright purchase or sale/repurchase dealings of the early 1960s. The reopening of a secondary market in government securities in 1966 following the introduction of a more active fiscal policy created wider scope for operations. Further diversification of instruments has been made in the more recent years, both with the introduction of the new system under which the central bank issues its own bills to mop up surplus funds from the money market and with the Bank's decision to carry out operations in the market for commercial and other bills.

b) *Changes in central bank lending*

While changes in the central bank's portfolio of securities — at least in the case of outright purchases and sales — affect the level of unborrowed reserves, changes in actual or potential lending by the central bank affect only borrowed or conditional reserves. It may be expected that the effects of the latter type of actions differ from those of varying the central bank's portfolio of securities in two ways:

i) they have a weaker impact on bank acquisitions of earning assets and on the money supply; and

ii) they have a weaker impact on rates on Treasury bills and other debt instruments in which open market operations take place.[2]

But the distinction between the effects of the two instruments must not be overdone; as the examples given above of reversible short-term transactions indicate, there are forms of open market operations which do not differ significantly from changes in central bank lending. There is clearly a high degree of substitution in the use of the two instruments; the larger the scope for flexible use of open market operations, the smaller are the adjustment burdens falling on variations in central bank lending.

The essential consideration in the evaluation of the rather different practices which have developed in the six countries is what determines the level of lending by the central bank to the private banks.[3] One extreme is a rationing system, in which the central bank makes available lending

---

1. OECD Monetary Studies Series, *Monetary Policy in France*, Part III.A.

2. In countries where both instruments have been used actively there appears to be evidence that the impact on interest rates is as strong (or even stronger) when central bank lending varies; the leading example is the Federal funds rate in the United States.

3. At times central banks lend, mainly for historical reasons, to other groups of financial institutions or even to the non-financial sector, but such lending is everywhere of limited and declining relative importance and will be disregarded in the following.

facilities more modest than those demanded by banks at the prevailing level of costs. The other is a system in which the central bank confines itself to setting the rate — or usually rates — at which it is prepared to lend, while the banks determine the extent to which the facilities are used. None of the six countries can be adequately described by either of these extremes, though Japan has over long periods been close to the former and Germany to the latter. In most countries, the *level* of central bank lending (or, synonymously, commercial bank borrowing) is, at any particular point of time, determined by the availability in recent periods of other sources of reserve money, which are largely a product of historical circumstances, institutional factors and traditions. Fluctuations around that level in normal times tend to reflect changes in the banks' demand for borrowed funds at the cost set by the central bank. In periods of monetary restraint this demand will obviously tend to shift upwards with the central bank aiming to curb the readiness of banks to borrow by a rise in its lending charges, a quantitative limitation of the facilities available, or possibly some combination of both. The differences among countries with respect to both the level of lending and its variability are quite striking. Measured in per cent of total deposits (Chart 7), the indebtedness of commercial banks is by far the highest in France and the lowest in the United States (and in the United Kingdom, which has been omitted from Chart 7, since there is no direct lending to the commercial banks). To the extent that there is an observable relationship between changes in lending and the introduction of restraint, it is that central bank lending tends to rise following the introduction of restraint. It is only in restrictive phases that banks make full use of their borrowing facilities, and even though the central bank may be curtailing them as part of its restrictive policies the observed volume of lending will often rise. A roughly similar pattern emerges when borrowing at the central bank is measured as a percentage of reserve money or monetary base (Chart 8), though the ranking of France and Japan is reversed.

To the extent that central bank lending is determined by the demand for reserves by banks, it is misleading to regard changes in lending as a policy instrument; changes in the cost of central bank funds — the discount rate and other lending rates — and in money market rates are a more direct expression of policy intent (Charts 9 and 10). Even in periods in which the central bank is aiming to ration its lending, it would be misleading to regard lending as fully subject to the discretion of the authorities. The central bank has a responsibility as a lender of last resort to provide the banks or other money market institutions with sufficient funds to prevent financial panics; this may force the hand of the monetary authorities to increase lending in the short run on some occasions when their slightly longer-run objectives would encourage more restraint. In any case, changes in lending have to be reviewed jointly with other sources of reserve money; if there is a very strong drain from one of these, e.g. because of the external deficit, the central bank may offset part of it through an increase of its lending. Another example is the pressure generated on banks' reserve positions by an increase in reserve requirement ratios which would at times become intolerable if the central bank were not prepared to help the banks through an adjustment period by permitting some increase in its lending; France is an example of such a partly-offsetting use of variations in central bank credit (page 39). As these illustrations show, the function of changes in central bank lending as a safety valve in balancing the market for reserve money precludes a direct interpretation of such changes as indications of policy intent.

Chart 7. BANK BORROWING AT THE CENTRAL BANK
Per cent of Resources

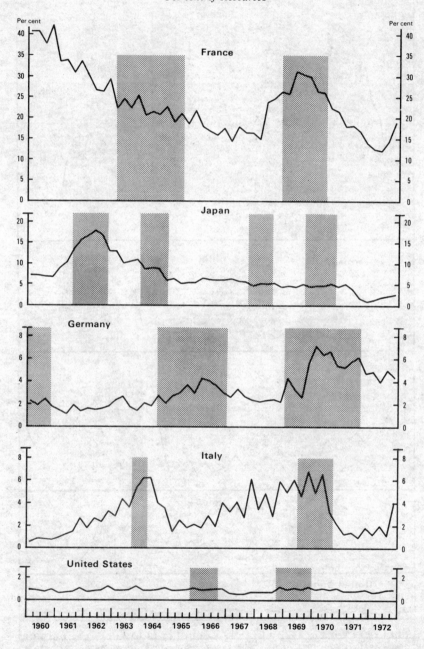

Chart 8. BANK BORROWING AT THE CENTRAL BANK
Per cent of Reserve Money

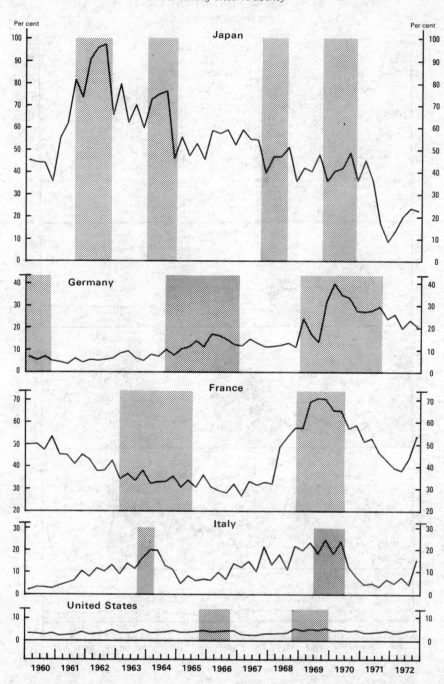

In *Japan,* changes in lending by the Bank of Japan have been a most important instrument for both long and short run changes in reserve money.[1] The dominant role of increases in central bank lending in gradually increasing the supply of reserve money was due to the limited availability of other major sources. The balance of payments on average remained near equilibrium until 1970. The central government aimed at balanced budgets up to the mid-1960s and subsequently at modest deficits financed by bond sales; there was very limited scope for substantially expansionary open market operations. In the face of these factors, there was a rapidly growing demand for reserve money. Though the increase in the demand for bank reserves was moderate because of low required reserve ratios, the demand for currency by the non-bank sector assumed very large proportions, with nominal incomes rising at a rate of more than 15 per cent per annum. The main way in which this longer-run tendency towards excess demand in the market for reserve money could be offset was to allow the major banks to increase their indebtedness to the Bank of Japan in line with the growth of their activity. However, in periods of restraint, individual banks' quotas for central bank borrowing could be lowered or credit denied to individual banks inside their specific quotas; variations in the basic discount rate were used to reinforce such rationing measures. The situation changed temporarily in 1971 when a huge external surplus reduced bank borrowing at the Bank of Japan sharply; but as the balance of payments surplus changed to deficit in 1972-73, borrowing has been restored almost to the level of the year 1970.

In *France* also, banks tended to rely heavily on central bank rediscount facilities until 1971 when Bank of France interventions in the money market gained importance as the source of central bank credit.[2] As in Japan, the banks operate at a very low level of excess reserves so that short-run fluctuations in the availability of reserves due to non-policy sources of supply or to the demand for currency outside banks have typically been offset by changes in central bank credit. Until 1972, rediscounting of eligible short-term paper was subject to quotas, and recourse above them was possible only at a penalty rate (until 1967, two penalty rates – the regular and higher penalty rates – were applicable according to the volume of borrowing above the quotas). Rediscounting of eligible medium-term paper has been limited by a ratio control which obliges the banks to maintain such a paper in their portfolio at least in a specified proportion to certain of their liabilities.[3] The basic discount rate has been changed with increasing frequency since 1968, and a number of other rates applying to the discounting of particular types of paper have been changed in step with it. While the effect on banks' willingness to extend credit of varying central bank lending rates has weakened since 1971 (when the central bank's intervention rate in the money market became the predominant determinant of the cost of reserve money), the authorities attach importance to the psychological effect of changes in the official discount rate.

In *Italy,* borrowing at the Bank of Italy was regulated primarily by rationing rather than by changes in cost; the discount rate was unchanged for 11 years prior to 1969.[4] Ceilings for individual bank borrowing in the

1. OECD Monetary Studies Series, *Monetary Policy in Japan,* pp. 25-26 and 73-78.
2. OECD Monetary Studies Series, *Monetary Policy in France,* Part III.A.
3. See *Ibid.,* for the earlier ratio control ("coefficient de trésorerie") in use between 1960 and 1967.
4. OECD Monetary Studies Series, *Monetary Policy in Italy, pp. 23-28, and 73-77.*

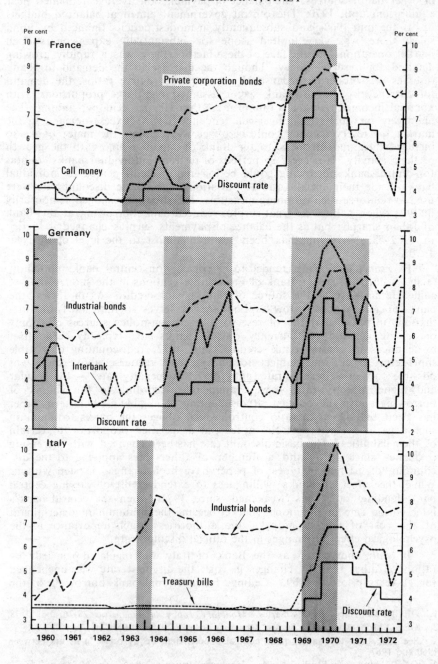

Chart 9. DISCOUNT RATES, OTHER SHORT-TERM RATES,
AND SELECTED LONGER-TERM RATES
FRANCE, GERMANY, ITALY

France

Private corporation bonds

Call money

Discount rate

Germany

Industrial bonds

Interbank

Discount rate

Italy

Industrial bonds

Treasury bills

Discount rate

1960 1961 1962 1963 1964 1965 1966 1967 1968 1969 1970 1971 1972

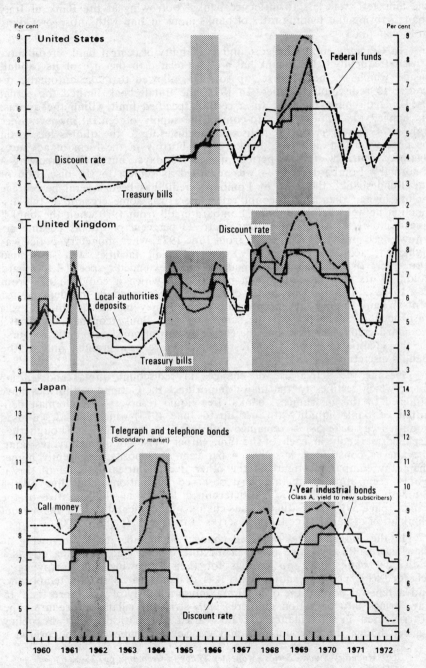

Chart 10. DISCOUNT RATES, OTHER SHORT-TERM RATES,
AND SELECTED LONGER-TERM RATES
UNITED STATES, UNITED KINGDOM, JAPAN

United States
Federal funds
Discount rate
Treasury bills

United Kingdom
Discount rate
Local authorities deposits
Treasury bills

Japan
Telegraph and telephone bonds
(Secondary market)
7-Year industrial bonds
(Class A, yield to new subscribers)
Call money
Discount rate

1960 1961 1962 1963 1964 1965 1966 1967 1968 1969 1970 1971 1972

form of advances on collateral were fixed at 3 to 5 per cent of deposits; in principle, credit inside the ceilings as well as rediscounting could be denied, but in practice these powers were not used. After 1969 the basic discount rate was changed a number of times, largely for external reasons; the aim here was less to influence banks' borrowing at the Bank of Italy than to bring the lending rates of banks more in line with those prevailing in foreign markets.

In *Germany*, both the cost and availability of central bank credit have varied frequently.[1] Each bank has a quota related to the size of its capital, inside which the banks were, up to 1973, allowed to make automatic recourse to rediscount facilities. In 1973, the Bundesbank limited the actual use of rediscount facilities to a certain specified limit within the quotas; it changed this limit at times to control the supply of central money. Since July 1974, however, use of rediscount facilities up to the quotas has again been allowed. In addition, banks could borrow in the form of advances against securities for a period up to 30 days, but such borrowing – "normal" Lombard credit – was regarded as subject to the discretion of the Bundesbank; the cost of Lombard credit has been several percentage points higher than the discount rate. There was some erosion of the distinction between rediscount and Lombard credit from 1970 when the banks' quasi-automatic use of the latter up to 20 per cent of quotas became acknowledged practice. With effect from June 1973, when monetary policy was tightened, access to "normal" Lombard credit facilities was suspended altogether. Instead, the Bundesbank at times extended "special" Lombard credit at its own discretion at a penalty rate which it could change from day to day. This type of credit, designed to accommodate the demand for central bank money in exceptionally tight money market conditions, was suspended in July 1974. At the same time, the Bank reopened "normal" Lombard credit facilities, but the earlier system of quasi-automatic recourse to the facilities has not been restored; they are now granted only at the Bank's discretion.

Despite the active use of changes in rediscount quotas and lending rates, which testifies to the major importance the German authorities have attached to this instrument, banks' free liquid reserves – the German definition of bank liquidity (in use up to June 1973) which includes unused quotas (see page 58) – remained substantial prior to 1973. Though they declined markedly in each of the three earlier phases of monetary restraint, they never constituted less than 4 per cent of deposits, apparently higher than any comparable figure in the other five countries. Because of this it would seem appropriate to regard observed fluctuations in lending by the Bundesbank prior to 1973 as determined largely at the initiative of the banks (page 59). The situation has changed fundamentally since the virtual elimination of banks' free liquid reserves in that year (pages 59-60).

In the *United States* observed changes in member bank borrowing at the Federal Reserve also reflect a mixture of cost and rationing effects.[2] Individual banks have no ceilings for their borrowing; but borrowing is regarded as a privilege, not a right. It is designed to be strictly temporary, and a renewal beyond the original maximum maturity of not more than 15 days brings into operation an increasingly strict surveillance procedure. The criteria used in surveillance are not varied systematically with the policy stance, though the discount rate may be. Several studies have uncovered a

1. *OECD Monetary Studies Series, Monetary Policy in Germany*, pp. 35-36.
2. OECD Monetary Studies Series, *Monetary Policy in the United States*, Part II.(c).

36

modest cost sensitivity in bank borrowing inside the range in which the majority of banks are not effectively restrained by the stricter surveillance of their respective Federal Reserve Bank. But in periods of monetary restraint such as 1966, 1969 and 1973 there is evidence that nominal cost considerations are no longer decisive; in the earlier two years, borrowing at the Federal Reserve did not rise sharply although the discount rate remained well below the rates observed in those parts of the money market which, to the individual bank, constitute alternative sources of funds – the Federal funds, Treasury bill and the Euro-dollar markets. Although the discount rate was changed more frequently in recent years, particularly in the expansionary phase of 1970–71 and again in the earlier part of the most recent restrictive phase, the dominant role of rationing elements appears to have been prevailing notably since mid-1973, despite the opening of additional seasonal facilities. The modest scale of borrowing is clearly not an indication that central bank policy in this area has been unimportant; on the contrary, the tight grip on borrowing and the relatively stable relation of total reserves to deposits (Chart 7) in the United States have tended to increase the importance of this instrument.

In the *United Kingdom,* central bank credit is of even smaller quantitative importance than in the United States. It is extended, not to the banks, but to the discount houses, which have obtained sole access to the lender of last resort facilities of the Bank of England in return for their undertaking to bid for the full weekly Treasury bill issue. Such lending is very short-term, never reaching more than a few per cent of discount house resources, and it would seem justified to conclude that it has played mainly a technical, smoothing role in United Kingdom monetary policy. Up to October 1972, depending on the option of the Bank, lending took place either at the going market rate or at the official discount rate (Bank rate) which was a penalty rate in that it remained above the return the discount houses could earn on most of their short-term assets. Since October 1972 the weekly announcement of Bank rate has been discontinued and its replacement, the Bank's Minimum Lending Rate, has normally been determined automatically by a formula which fixes it slightly higher than the average discount rate for Treasury bills.[1] But a change in the lending rate independent of this arrangement has not been excluded. In fact, towards the end of 1973 the Minimum Lending Rate was raised by the discretion of the monetary authorities to a level well above the going bill rate in order to ease the downward pressure on sterling in exchange markets.

c) *Changes in minimum reserve requirements*

Variation of minimum reserve requirement ratios against bank deposits (or possibly bank loans) is the third major instrument available in all six countries. It has been used with greatly varying intensity and has been important throughout the period under study only in Germany; it appears to have come increasingly into use in the United Kingdom, France and Japan. Reserve requirement ratios may be defined in a number of ways. The denominator may not comprise all deposits; it may distinguish among different categories, notably by maturity as in the United States or according to the status of the depositor (resident or non-resident). The numerator may comprise a more or less wide range of liquid assets, from non-interest bearing deposits with the central bank to short-term marketable government

1. One-half per cent above the average discount rate for Treasury bills at the most recent tender, rounded to the nearest one-fourth per cent above.

37

debt. There is also wider scope for more technical variations in setting up the rules for computing and observing the requirements and for the sanctions to be imposed in cases of non-compliance.

In its classical form, in which reserve requirement ratios are applied to the level of broad categories of deposits, and reserves are to be held in non-interest-bearing accounts at the central bank, the instrument is one that will powerfully affect the excess and net free reserves of the banks and thereby lead to a contraction of the lending capacity of the banking system. The basic philosophy is that banks can satisfy the need for additional reserves imposed by a rise in the ratios only by acquiring earning assets at a slower rate (possibly negative) than they would have otherwise. This presupposes that banks cannot in other ways supply themselves with all or most of the reserves impounded by the higher ratios, i.e. that the supply of reserve money is effectively controlled by the authorities.

In view of the discontinuous nature of the variations — ratios are rarely changed by less than one or possibly one-half percentage point — it has been argued that the instrument will often be too blunt to be used in normal circumstances. If the level of excess reserves is very low, there will be room for increases in the required ratios only if the central bank is prepared to supply additional reserves through open market operations or by lending, thereby offsetting some of the restrictive impact. Such a combination of partially offsetting measures may at times be found desirable in the light of complex objectives with respect to both liquidity and interest rates. Otherwise the main use of variations in reserve requirement ratios is for neutralizing large changes in bank liquidity arising from non-controlled sources of reserve creation, normally external surpluses or deficits; Germany is the leading example of such use of the instrument. In countries where the relative size of such uncontrolled disturbances is modest and where the use of the instrument can therefore be geared to domestic objectives, variations in reserve requirement ratios would seem to have their main comparative advantage relatively early in upswings and downswings; both the need and the scope for restrictive or expansionary measures are particularly large at such times. But requirements may be — and have in fact been — raised late in a boom or in countries where banks at all times operate at very low levels of excess reserves, provided the central bank is prepared to let banks borrow to meet (some of) the additional requirements. To that extent, there will be no multiplier effect of the increase, but only a cost effect.

The bluntness of the instrument will be strongly modified if the reserve requirements apply only to certain categories of volatile deposits, such as those held by non-residents, or to increases in deposits (or lending) beyond a base date. Such marginal reserve requirement ratios have become more frequently employed in recent years as a supplement to existing, and typically much lower, average ratios. Another recent tendency in some countries is to apply the requirements to increases in lending rather than in deposits. This is thought to make individual banks more conscious of policy intentions. The level of loan commitments is the main strategic variable to a bank, whereas deposits are only very indirectly controlled; the impact on bank behaviour may be reinforced when the changes in reserve requirements enter directly into the marginal calculations of extending loans.

The *German* monetary authorities have undoubtedly made most important use of this instrument; reserve requirements ratios have been varied more than 30 times since 1960. Incremental requirements have been applied almost exclusively to non-resident deposits, at times as much as 100 per cent. During the three phases of restraint prior to 1973, increases in reserve requirement ratios were the main sources of policy-induced changes in bank liquidity.[1] No interest is paid on required reserves, and a penalty rate of 3 percentage points above the discount rate is charged on shortfalls; on the other hand, the method of compiling the requirement leaves individual banks some flexibility in temporarily drawing down reserves. The Bundesbank in 1972 proposed new legislation that would empower it to require reserves to be held also against increases in lending,[2] but it is as yet uncertain whether such legislation would be passed by the Bundestag.

In *France* variations in reserve requirement ratios have been made frequently since 1967 when the banks' liquid assets other than medium-term discountable paper were exempted from minimum ratio controls.[3] Two main motives have guided the use of the instrument: *i*) to influence the banks' reliance on central bank credit, and thereby to reinforce the impact on banks' lending rates arising from a more flexible use of central bank lending rates since 1967; and *ii*) to offset, primarily since 1971, the impact of capital flows on bank liquidity. Initially, the ratios applied only to deposits, but since 1971 they have been supplemented by ratios against increases in lending. Since 1972 banks have been made subject to progressively higher requirements which can be applied to the total of their lending if it accelerates beyond the rate of increase recommended by the Bank of France. This new arrangement tends to make the authorities' control on bank lending as effective as direct ceilings (page 41).[4]

In the *United Kingdom* two conventional ratios were for a long time thought to constitute a fulcrum for the actions of the monetary authorities: one of cash to deposits of 8 per cent and one of a broader range of liquid assets to deposits of initially 30 and subsequently 28 per cent. Both of these applied only to clearing banks and were based on a gentlemen's agreement rather than banking legislation. On top of this, at times of restraint since 1959, the Bank of England has made calls for "Special Deposits" into interest-bearing accounts with it, typically in steps of 1 per cent of clearing bank deposits. Following the introduction of the new arrangements for *Competition and Credit Control,* the major reform of 1971, a uniform ratio of 12.5 per cent of "eligible reserve assets" to specified liabilities was introduced for all banks (10 per cent for finance houses). This ratio is also based on a gentlemen's agreement and not on statutory powers. The assets eligible as reserves can to some extent be produced through transactions between the banks and the discount houses; bank loans to the latter qualify as reserves, part of which the discount houses are able to redeposit with the banks.[5] The Bank of England in 1973 eliminated some of this scope

1. OECD Monetary Studies Series, *Monetary Policy in Germany*, Charts 12-14.
2. The change in legislation requiring interest-free deposits with the Bundesbank on non-bank inflows of funds is reviewed on page 49.
3. For details of the new system, see page 33 of the text, and OECD Monetary Studies Series, *Monetary Policy in France*, Part III, A.
4. *Ibid.*
5. The definition of eligible reserve assets falls between the traditional concepts of cash and liquid assets (see *Competition and Credit Control*, Bank of England, 1971). It comprises: central bank balances, Treasury bills, tax reserve certificates, call loans (primarily to the discount houses), government or government-guaranteed bonds with at most one year to final maturity, local authority bills and commercial bills (at most 2 per cent of deposits). Changes in the definition are explained in *Bank of England Quarterly Bulletin*, September 1973, pp. 306-307.

for offsets to monetary policy actions through firmer regulation of the activities of the discount houses; this also had the effect of reducing distortions in short-term money markets. After a period of adjustment in 1971–72, banks' reserve asset ratios fell to a level slightly above the prescribed minimum. In the restrictive policy period of 1973, calls for special deposits played an important role in reducing the actual ratio. The Government withdrew interest payments on the proportion of special deposits related to banks' non-interest-bearing liabilities in October 1973. The withdrawal was wholly aimed at reducing an element of bank profit and was not a credit control measure. It may be noted that deposits under the " supplementary scheme " (page 43) also do not carry interest to reinforce the cost restraint on the attraction of additional deposits.

In the three remaining countries the instrument has been used much less frequently. The Bank of *Japan* has changed the comparatively low reserve requirement ratios cyclically since September 1959.[1] Until 1971 the need for restrictive action of this kind was limited by the heavy dependence of the banks on borrowing at the Bank of Japan. Prior to 1972, requirements applied only to residents' yen deposits; subsequently the Bank of Japan has been empowered to extend them (and to apply percentages up to 100) to banks' liabilities vis-à-vis non-residents. In 1973 requirements were introduced against bank debentures and trust funds. In *Italy,* reserve requirement ratios have only once been changed across the board. This change as well as subsequent redefinitions of the eligible assets were in the direction of ease and designed to encourage an active role for banks and savings banks in the bond market; banks may now hold part, savings banks all, of their required reserves in the form of bonds. In mid-1973 the Italian monetary authorities went considerably further in this direction by requesting the commercial banks to hold government and private bonds at least in an amount equivalent to 6 per cent (9 per cent for the first half of 1974, and 12 per cent for the second half), of their deposits at end-1972. The structural aim of rechannelling part of the credit flows via the bond market and keeping the long-term bond rate as low and stable as possible was once more emphasized.[2] In the *United States* there also has been only limited use of the instrument for short-term stabilization, though it has long existed and can be varied within wide limits. Ratios were pushed near to their maxima during World War II and subsequently reduced during the 1940s and 1950s to a level probably not far above what banks might in any case have been willing to hold. Since 1960 the ratios have been varied less; they were raised in 1969 and changed in both directions in 1973. In 1969 differential requirements on bank borrowings in the Euro-dollar market were imposed for the first time. In 1972 the very complex definitions used were simplified by eliminating geographical location. Still the instrument is unlikely to become the major one, partly because it is considered too blunt (see page 38), partly because of the risk that member banks might disaffiliate in greater numbers from the Federal Reserve System ; it is thought that one major reason behind the observed decline in the number of member banks is that non-member banks are often subject to lower requirements by the states in which they operate.[3]

1. OECD Monetary Studies Series, *Monetary Policy in Japan*, pp. 27-28 and 78-79.
2. OECD Monetary Studies Series, *Monetary Policy in Italy*, pp. 23-24 and 67-70. For an analysis of developments in 1973 see also OECD, *Economic Survey of Italy*, December 1973, Part II. The Italian measures are not, strictly speaking, reserve requirements, but rather a constraint on banks' choice among earning assets.
3. OECD, Monetary Studies Series, *Monetary Policy in the United States*, Part II.(e).

d)   *Ceilings on bank lending and other financial flows*

The three main instruments surveyed above are the only measures which have been used in all of the six countries at one time or another. There are, however, important additional instruments in use in some of the countries, the most important of which is the fixing of ceilings to the lending by banks and at times by specialized financial institutions and to the issue of bonds. The main purpose here is not to review selective measures of credit control, such as rationing — or, more likely, preferential treatment — of, say, mortgage finance, though some comments will be made on major examples of such attempts by countries in the review of the impact on financial variables below. Here the use of ceilings as a general instrument in stabilization policy is to be reviewed.

A main purpose of ceilings is to improve the accuracy and speed with which the monetary authorities can influence bank lending and the money supply. It is probably beyond dispute that ceilings have some such advantage in the short run over the indirect instruments described above. The issues are then: *1*) whether the greater degree of control over particular financial flows has a counterpart in significantly different effects on the real economy; and *2*) whether there are disadvantages associated with ceilings which outweigh the possible gains in precision. The answers to these two questions remain highly provisional and depend to a large extent on the length of time ceilings are kept in existence. The experiences in the six countries range widely; only two of them — the United States and Germany — have made no use of ceilings, but in Germany the authority to impose ceilings on bank lending was contained in new legislative proposals that were under active consideration in the Bundestag in 1973. Of the other four countries, the United Kingdom abandoned a comprehensive system of ceilings in 1971; Italy recently introduced them for the first time on some types of bank lending, in addition to ceiling controls on bond issues which have been in use for some time; Japan and France have made extensive use of the instrument.

In *Japan* ceilings have been used frequently as a supplement to the main traditional approach of varying credit from the Bank of Japan.[1] At first ceilings were fixed monthly, later quarterly; they were aimed mainly at the large city banks, but more recently extended also to other banks. For about two years from late 1968 the system was replaced by regulation of the liquidity position of commercial banks. In early 1973, the Bank reintroduced credit ceilings. In order to minimize the disadvantages in terms of limiting competition in the banking sector, the Bank has refrained from rigidly similar treatment of the controlled banks. In fixing individual banks' ceilings in 1967 for example, the Bank favoured those that borrowed the least from the Bank and the money market. Commercial banks closely observed ceiling controls which were supported by the Bank's strong position as the creditor to them, and no sanctions were considered necessary in Japan.

In *France* ceilings on bank lending were the dominant instrument in the two periods of monetary restraint up to 1970. They were typically used selectively; in 1968-1970, lending to exporters was exempted from ceilings, and discountable medium-term credits to fixed investment were allowed to expand faster than the remaining two-thirds of bank credit. The authorities employed some sanctions to secure compliance with ceiling

---

1.   OECD Monetary Studies Series, *Monetary Policy in Japan*, pp. 28-29, 81-82.

controls. Initially, the penalty involved only reduction of the offending banks' rediscounting facilities with the Bank of France. During 1969, bank lending subject to the ceilings continued to exceed the limits and individual banks were therefore penalized. As this type of penalty proved inadequate,[1] in the spring of 1970 the offending banks were required to make non-interest-bearing deposits, equivalent to a certain proportion of the excess credit, with the Bank of France. In view of the experiences of disinter-mediation — bank depositors and borrowers being brought in direct contact by the banks outside the reach of the ceilings — and the apparent loss of efficiency in the financial sector due to diminished competition, the French authorities consider the instrument to be useable only in exceptional cir-cumstances. The earlier system of credit ceilings is not relied upon in the present phase of monetary restraint. Instead, recommended rates of increase of bank lending have been announced by the authorities, and those banks which accelerate lending above the guidelines are subject to highly progressive reserve requirements which are applied to the total of their lending (i.e. not to the excess lending). In addition to credit ceilings, regulations on consumer credit have at times been made, notably in the form of controls on the minimum amount of down-payments in hire pur-chases of consumer durables and the maximum length of repayment periods.

In the *United Kingdom,* ceilings in specific forms were first established in 1965 (on earlier occasions, the authorities asked for credit restriction without indicating quantitative limits). They were applied to all banks and major hire-purchase finance houses. After the discontinuation of ceilings on major commercial banks' lending for a short period in 1967, all banks and major finance houses were subject to direct controls with some modifi-cations from late 1967 until 1971. Ceilings were normally fixed as a per-centage of loans outstanding in a base period. The Bank of England in the absence of statutory powers relied on voluntary co-operation for im-plementation of the programme. But, because the clearing banks *as a group* remained over their ceilings in the early months of 1969, in May 1969, as a penal measure, the rate of interest payable on special deposits (page 39) was halved. One of the problems with credit ceilings came from the British banking practice of allowing customers agreed overdraft limits (which are often more important in their availability than in their use) and the difficulty in predicting the extent to which customers will take up the limits already agreed. The quantitative ceilings were accompanied by quali-tative guidance on the direction of lending. The authorities accorded priority to finance for production and investment necessary to sustain or increase exports, for the promotion of invisible earnings, or for securing a saving in imports. At the same time, the banks and major finance houses were asked to restrict non-priority lending, such as credits for imports and per-sonal spending. There can be little doubt, in the light of the explosive growth of this non-priority lending following the removal of ceilings in 1971, that at least such lending was held back during the period of the ceilings. The main reason for the reform embarked upon in the Bank of England's *Competition and Credit Control* was a concern that the efficiency of the institutions affected has become increasingly hamstrung by the lack of competition imposed by the ceilings; the timing of the reform was con-

---

1. The interest differential between the discount rate and the money market rate was not large enough to discourage the banks whose rediscount quotas had been reduced from making up for the loss in liquidity by obtaining funds in the money market where the Bank of France stood ready to meet residual demand for funds.

ditioned by the need for a more expansionary policy stance following the emergence of slack in the United Kingdom economy in 1970–71 and the strong recovery of the external balance.

Despite a rate of growth of bank lending and money supply generally recognized to be excessive in the light of developments in the external balance, the exchange rate and the domestic price level, there was no attempt to return to quantitative controls on bank lending or other monetary aggregates prior to late 1973; the emphasis in monetary policy remained on increases in interest rates and calls for Special Deposits. A noticeable change took place in September 1973 when banks were asked in qualitative form to restrain the provision of credit to persons, property development and financial transactions.[1] In December 1973 minimum down-payments and maximum repayment periods were reimposed on hire purchasers; such regulations had been used frequently in the 1960s, but they were scrapped in 1971 around the time when Competition and Credit Control was put into effect. Finally, in December 1973, the Bank of England introduced the "supplementary scheme" which sets a guideline for the rate of growth of interest-bearing eligible liabilities of banks and deposit-taking finance houses and requires non-interest-bearing Supplementary Special Deposits to be placed with the Bank of England if the guideline is exceeded.[2] The effect of the scheme is to increase progressively the marginal cost of usable funds to the banks; if the guideline is exceeded by more than 3 per cent, the marginal cost of usable funds is of the order of 40 per cent. The scheme is similar in some respect to the reserve requirements against increases in lending above the growth rate recommended by the authorities in France (pages 39 and 41); but the U.K. scheme was designed to leave more freedom to the banks to arrange their asset portfolios and to give a higher degree of control over the money stock. The scheme was extended in April 1974 for a further six month period.

In *Italy* direct controls were limited, prior to 1973, to fund flows through specialized institutions and issues of securities. Though the control of issues has at times been used counter-cyclically, notably in 1969–1970, the main purpose of intervention has been of a structural nature, viz. to improve the geographical or sectoral allocation of resources or, more narrowly, the technical functioning of the bond market.[3] But in July 1973 when bank lending accelerated, partly at the expense of bank purchases of bonds, the Bank of Italy acted to limit directly the growth of banks' short-term lending to larger borrowers and to certain other sectors (about two-thirds of total short-term loans outstanding). This step constituted part of a large number of measures to dampen domestic inflation and an outflow of capital which was putting severe downward pressure on the lira.[4] It is as yet too early to say whether the use of ceilings on bank lending marks a switch towards instruments which work more directly on an important policy target or a response specifically designed to meet the rather exceptional circumstances since 1973.

1. Letter from the Governor in *Bank of England Quarterly Bulletin*, December 1973, p. 445.
2. The scheme is described in detail in *Ibid.*, March and June 1974.
3. OECD Monetary Studies Series, *Monetary Policy in Italy*, pp. 11-21.
4. For a more detailed description of the measures, see OECD Economic Surveys, *Italy*, December 1973.

In conclusion, this survey of the attitude towards ceilings as an important policy instrument suggests that with the exception of the United States, where the structure of the banking system makes the instrument impractical, the question of future use of ceilings is unsettled. Japan and France have found it difficult to dispense with ceilings, though in France a close substitute in the form of marginal reserve requirements against lending appears to have been found. A substitute was also actively considered in Germany in 1973. Italy also seems to have moved in the direction of ceilings. The United Kingdom appeared to be an important exception, a tendency which may not be unrelated to the fact that the degree of resource utilization in the U.K. economy left more room for expansionary policies than was the case in most other economies since 1971; the U.K. authorities aimed to preserve the scope for a differential monetary policy through the floating of sterling since June 1972 and by preserving tight controls on residents' capital transactions overseas. When external developments became alarming in 1973, the authorities first relied on interest rates rather than ceilings. But later in 1973, the U.K. moved some way towards reliance on more direct methods of influencing the monetary aggregates and reimposed elements of qualitative guidance on bank lending and hire purchase regulations (page 43). In circumstances not very dissimilar, Italy, which had also through floating aimed to preserve a policy stance more expansionary than the average, chose to rely on both increases in short-term domestic interest rates and the imposition of ceilings on bank lending. In contrast to the United Kingdom, where control of residents' external transactions is more effective, direct controls on bank lending in Italy were motivated by external considerations to stem capital outflows.

e) *Administrative controls on interest rates*

In a number of cases administrative controls over selected interest rates supplement the indirect influence exercised through variations of central bank lending rates and purchases or sales of securities. The motives for retaining such controls are complex and partly conflicting, but three main motives seem to emerge. They may all be reviewed in the light of regulations in existence in the *United States*:

　　i) a bias in favour of low interest rates, particularly those charged to public borrowers and to private borrowers for purposes enjoying political favour.

This motive underlies the retention of ceilings on the coupon rates which may be offered on Treasury longer-term debt issues and on the rates which may be charged to some categories of housebuilding (veterans housing, social housing). This motive is on the wane because strict application of it leads to the choking off of funds to those borrowers which the rate ceilings were designed to protect.

　　ii) A desire to prevent sudden shifts of funds in response to interest rate differentials between various kinds of financial assets held by households and non-financial firms.

This motive is illustrated by the maximum on rates offered on smaller (i.e. less than $100,000) deposits in banks and savings institutions under Regulation Q. In periods of rising interest rates the savings and loan associations and the mutual savings banks found it difficult to offer competitive rates because their assets were tied up in loans contracted at the lower interest rates prevailing prior to the mid-1960s. In the absence of the Regulation Q maxima on rates offered to commercial bank depositors, the savings institutions and their borrowers (largely in the housing sector) would have been drained of funds to an undesirable extent. The urgency of using administrative controls as a protection against financial instability is weakening because of the increasing ability of the savings institutions to adjust the rates on their outstanding loans. Mainly for this reason the application of Regulation Q to smaller deposits was more flexible in 1973 than in the earlier periods of tight money; however, Congress did act to insure that ceilings would apply to the rates offered by commercial banks on special 4-year deposits, thus aiming to preserve the competitiveness of non-bank institutions.

iii) A desire to influence the lending potential of banks by impeding their ability to retain large deposits (mainly from corporations) in periods of rising market interest rates.

This was the rationale of the application of Regulation Q to deposits larger than $100,000. However, during the two restrictive phases in 1966 and 1969 during which these maxima were effective — i.e. when rates on competing market instruments rose above them — banks were able to protect their lending, at least their business and industrial loans, by tapping untraditional sources of funds domestically or in the Euro-dollar market and by selling short-term securities. These possibilities for offset plus disturbances in financial markets (notably the crisis in the commercial paper market at the time of Penn Central's financial difficulties) associated with the large-scale disintermediation in periods of monetary restraint contributed to the suspension of ceilings on large deposits of 30-89 days' maturity in 1970. The ceilings on large deposits have subsequently been fully suspended.

This survey of the rationale for administrative controls over interest rates suggests that, at least in the United States, time is working in favour of their abolition. A diminishing degree of specialization among financial institutions, greater flexibility in the lending rates charged by savings institutions and the growing scope for disintermediation all point in this direction. Financial markets in the United States have reached such a state of integration that administrative controls over price formation in selected sub-markets tend to become self-defeating. The stage during which sharply fluctuating money market rates coexisted uneasily with sluggish or administratively limited bank interest rates appears to have come near to its end during the 1960s and early 1970s as intensive competition for funds among banks in the market for certificates of deposit and greater flexibility in lending arrangements, e.g. through floating prime rates and variable mortgage rates, spread through the system. The United States experiences suggest that the situation in which administrative controls over deposit rates can make their maximum contribution as an instrument of monetary policy is that in which deposits are close substitutes both for deposits in other financial institutions and for money market assets, but in which banks have a greater ability to compete with money market rates than other depository institutions. The analyses of other countries may proceed by examining the extent to which these conditions have been met.

The *United Kingdom* is in a position not very dissimilar to that of the United States: there are highly developed markets in a number of short-term financial assets — notably local authority and central government debt instruments and sterling certificates of deposit — in which U.K. firms and wealthy individuals participate actively, though the dominant transactors are banks and other financial intermediaries. There is also a wide range of non-sterling assets available to non-residents. Interest rates in these markets move over an increasingly wide range and banks have been compelled to compete by increasing flexibility in the determination of their interest rates. Under *Competition and Credit Control*, introduced in 1971, clearing banks abandoned the cartel arrangement which tied their lending and deposit rates with Bank rate, and started to determine individually their base rate for lending and deposits, taking into account the development of money market rates. On the other hand, the terms offered by another category of financial institution, the building societies, deposits in which are close substitutes for bank deposits, have remained rather rigid. The reason is not that their lending rates are necessarily fixed – mortgage rates may be varied – but that administrative guidance and other complications have tended to limit the frequency with which interest rate changes can be undertaken. In periods of rising rates it has proved difficult to preserve stable inflows of funds into building society deposits and thereby a desirable minimum degree of availability of housing finance. The authorities took special measures to mitigate this problem in 1972–73; first by granting the building societies a temporary subsidy[1] and later, in September 1973, by fixing a limit on the rate which banks may pay on smaller (less than £10,000) deposits. This is a use of administrative controls closely analogous to the application of Regulation Q to smaller deposits in the United States, as described on page 44(*ii*) above.

In *Germany* as in the United Kingdom, cartel agreements in the banking sector effectively assured that changes in the discount rate were quickly and fully reflected in the rates charged and paid by banks. Such a situation offered advantages to the authorities to the extent that changes in these rates were thought to be an important influence on spending or capital flows; and it gave them a major weapon to affect bank deposits to the extent that they could vary interest rates on short-term instruments, which are substitutes for bank deposits, independently, thereby creating incentives for larger shifts in and out of bank deposits and reserves. Nevertheless, competition in the setting of interest rates has been encouraged since 1967 because of the expected beneficial effects on efficiency in the banking sector. A similar process could be observed in *Italy* from the late 1960s, though there was no clear official encouragement. In 1966, the *French* authorities also abolished administrative controls on banks' minimum lending rates, which had been modified generally in response to changes in the official discount rate. While bank deposit rates have continued to be stringently controlled by the authorities, they have been modified more flexibly since the mid-1960s. On the other hand, the *Japanese* authorities have maintained ceiling controls on banks' lending and deposit rates. Within the administered maximum limits, the banks' prime lending rate has been varied with changes in the official discount rate, but other lending rates have not automatically followed suit. As for bank deposit rates, they have been actually maintained at the administered maximum levels which have been rarely modified during the period under review. In both France and Japan, yields on new issues of long-term private bonds have been determined by issuers in close consultation with the authorities. Some countries also exercise administrative controls over or subsidize selected interest rates, typically lending rates of specialized credit institutions, to favour the

1. A loan extended by the authorities to the societies in 1974 was also aimed at keeping their interest rates down (footnote 2 on page 82).

allocation of funds to sectors considered of high social priority; important examples are the subsidized rates on loans for regional development purposes in Italy and France.

The practical effect of abolishing administrative controls on interest rates may not have been very great; there is evidence that banks continue to take discount rate changes as a signal to modify their own rates. In any case the willingness on the part of the monetary authorities to engage in open competition with the banks for the funds of depositors, or at least to allow such competition through market instruments, was mainly a feature of the United States scene, though there have been signs in 1973 of a growing willingness on the part of the Bundesbank to provide direct acquisition by the non-bank sector of securities, i.e. "disintermediation". But the authorities in some countries, of which Italy may recently have offered the clearest example, have found it convenient to retain some control over bank lending rates because such a control facilitates desired substitution between domestic bank financing on the one hand and domestic long-term or foreign financing on the other. The scope for twisting the structure of interest rates is greater in a system in which a high degree of control over bank lending rates is retained.

f) *Controls on foreign transactions of banks and non-banks*

All six countries have used either formal rules or informal guidance to influence the foreign transactions of banks. There is a wide variety of such controls currently in existence; between 1971 (the terminal year in the review of policies in individual countries) and late 1973 they multiplied in the wake of the increasing volatility of short-term capital flows. Most of these controls were designed to limit inflows or encourage outflows; they comprise, *inter alia,* discriminatory reserve requirements against foreign liabilities, swap arrangements at preferential rates between the central bank and the commercial banks and a number of non-price measures such as prescriptions for banks' net foreign position and ceilings on interest payments on non-resident accounts (usually zero or even negative). Germany has extended these measures to non-banks from 1972 through the imposition of deposit requirements against most forms of non-bank borrowing abroad and by limiting severely the scope for non-resident purchases of domestic bonds. Three countries have primarily been concerned to limit outflows of funds: Italy, the United Kingdom and the United States, which have all at times experienced large short-term capital exports. The main instruments have again been regulation of banks' net foreign position, outright prohibition of a number of non-bank transactions and the setting up of a special exchange market for capital transactions in which the domestic currency is allowed to depreciate.

The diversity of these measures is clearly very great, and attempts to co-ordinate them internationally or regionally, in the case of Member countries in the European Communities, have not yielded results. Yet this basic purpose can be briefly summarized despite the numerous and complex characteristics. It is to reduce, in the limit to eliminate, the sensitivity of capital flows to shifts in relative monetary conditions and in exchange-rate expectations and thereby the complications that arise in managing domestic reserve money. Some comments on the sensitivity of capital flows in individual countries are made below in Part III.B. While the experience of countries has differed widely, partly as a result of their attitude to capital controls, they have all at times been faced with the problem of reconciling

47

internal and external objectives. The possibility suggested by theoretical considerations of assigning monetary policy to the external and fiscal policy to the internal objective(s) has often been unfeasible either because the fiscal instruments have not been sufficiently flexible or because the impact of changes in traditional instruments of monetary policy on capital flows has been too imprecise. In such circumstances it has seemed much simpler to regulate capital flows directly, thereby preserving some scope for use of monetary policy for internal objectives.

Throughout the period covered systematically by the individual country studies, i.e. 1960–1971, the international monetary system was based on a system of fixed parities around which only very limited fluctuations in exchange rates were allowed. The extension of the bands of permissible fluctuations to 2.25 per cent of the parities or central rates agreed upon at the Smithsonian Institute in December 1971 was designed to restore a larger measure of monetary independence. The short duration of the new pattern of rates and the difficulties of keeping market rates near the centre of the wider bands made the implications of this experience for internal monetary policy inconclusive. In April 1972 the mark, French franc, pound sterling and lira narrowed their scope for fluctuations under the so-called "snake" arrangement together with other currencies in the European Communities. But from June 1972 sterling was allowed to float individually, and the lira followed a similar course from early 1973. The yen was set on a course of managed floating from February 1973. Sudden adjustments of the dollar exchange rates of both the yen and the mark were also made subsequently. In early 1974, the French franc started to float independently of the remaining currencies in the joint EEC float. Although the system of unprecedented flexibility of all important exchange rates led to a higher degree of monetary independence, the panoply of measures undertaken to restrict capital flows suggests that independence remained limited. As all of the six countries have seen their current balances worsen since late 1973 as a result of the oil price increases, the emphasis in some of them on limiting inflows is disappearing. It seems as yet too early to analyse these issues systematically.

Controls have tended to be the most comprehensive in *Japan*.[1] A major instrument has been regulation of the excess of the banks' total foreign currency liabilities plus some liabilities in domestic currency over the sum of all categories of foreign currency assets. In restrictive periods, this so-called "Yen conversion restriction measure" and several other forms of administrative controls were used to prevent banks from offsetting domestic monetary restraint by foreign borrowing. Flows of non-bank capital were also regulated through close supervision of long-term capital movements, both direct and portfolio, and through narrower limits than in any of the other countries studied on the scope for varying the patterns of payments for imports and exports – leads and lags. Subsequently, particularly in 1971, even these measures proved inadequate to stem an inflow of funds in anticipation of a yen revaluation.

In some respects the methods used in *Italy* have resembled those relied upon in Japan.[2] Regulation of the net foreign position of the banks was used very actively to limit the impact of the 1962–63 boom and the subsequent downswing on Italy's official international reserves. Controls on non-bank flows have been less frequent and less effective. The large current

1. OECD Monetary Studies Series, *Monetary Policy in Japan*, pp. 29 and 83-85.
2. OECD Monetary Studies Series, *Monetary Policy in Italy*, pp. 24-25 and 71-73.

surplus for a long span of years from 1964–65 allowed a substantial capital outflow. But some steps were taken to check the outflow. Purchase of repatriated lira notes was centralized in the Bank of Italy and from 1972 the rate on such notes was allowed to depreciate, thereby limiting an outflow of funds which had reached excessive proportions. From early 1973 a separate exchange market for capital transactions was set up, and the financial lira has since been quoted at a discount. This market was discontinued in early 1974.

In *France,* a mixture of direct regulations and price incentives has been used to limit inflows and at times outflows.[1] Controls were largely suppressed between the end of 1966 and the summer of 1968, and subsequent reinforcements have concentrated on the prevention of short-term inflows. The major instruments have been the prohibition of interest payments to non-residents' deposits, regulation of banks' net position, and, since August 1971, the separation of the exchange market into a managed market for commercial transactions and a free market for capital transactions (and selected current transactions). The maximum spread between the financial franc rate and the commercial rate tended to remain within a range of 4-5 per cent, even in periods of great uncertainties about the future course of the commercial franc. This suggests that there has been some scope for arbitrage transactions between the two markets. In early 1974 after the commercial franc was allowed to float individually, the financial franc market was scrapped.

The *German* authorities have, in fact, during most of the period since 1960, aimed at influencing the net foreign position of the banks.[2] The preferred instrument was the provision of swap facilities against dollars at rates more favourable than those available in the free market, i.e. encouraging the banks to place abroad a large part of any inflow of funds. Discriminatory reserve requirements against non-resident deposits and increases in such deposits have been applied on a number of occasions. Restrictions on interest payments on non-residents' deposits and sale of domestic money market paper have also been used frequently. Since 1964 a number of other measures have gradually come into effect applying to non-banks as well. In that year, the government announced a coupon tax on non-residents' holdings of bonds to limit capital inflows in this form; it was introduced in 1965. As measures relying on financial disincentives proved inadequate to check inflows induced by revaluation expectations, the acceptance of deposits from non-residents was subjected to licensing for a short period from late 1968. In 1972, the sale of domestic bonds to non-residents was also made subject to licensing; in the subsequent year, control was extended to other types of securities. The most remarkable system, and one that so far exists only in Germany, is the 1972 Cash Deposits Scheme (Bardepot) which requires companies to deposit a certain percentage (initially 40 per cent, 50 per cent from June 1973, 20 per cent from February 1974 and zero since September 1974) of the proceeds of foreign borrowing in non-interest-bearing accounts at the Bundesbank, thereby effectively manipulating the cost to enterprises. Finally, Germany has on two occasions — in 1969 and 1971 — resorted to individual floating to limit the inflow of funds. Though the range of instruments differs from that used in the other major countries, mainly by relying relatively more heavily on a price mech-

1. OECD Monetary Studies Series, *Monetary Policy in France*, Part III.A.
2. OECD Monetary Studies Series, *Monetary Policy in Germany*, pp. 38-39.

anism than on administrative controls, this enumeration underlines the importance which capital controls have come to play among the instruments of monetary policy in Germany.

In the two remaining countries the emphasis has been on the limitation of outflows. In the *United Kingdom,* a main instrument has been to oblige residents wishing to undertake portfolio investment outside the sterling area to obtain their foreign exchange in a separate market for investment currency in which the premium has since the mid-1960s fluctuated between 20 and 35 per cent (a peak of 50 per cent was reached in 1969 and again in 1974). From 1961–62 a similar procedure was prescribed for direct investment overseas outside the sterling area to the extent that such investment could not be financed out of the proceeds of foreign borrowing. Main categories of sterling area transactions became subject to licensing in the mid-1960s, and when exchange controls were tightened in June 1972 most remaining preferences for sterling area transactions were largely eliminated. From March 1974 direct investment in the overseas sterling area has been put on the same footing as other U.K. investment overseas. The flow of banking funds has been regulated mainly through ceilings on individual banks' overall open position in foreign currencies and on the amount of spot assets which may be held against forward liabilities in foreign currencies.

In the *United States* the first measure to limit outflows was taken in 1963 with the announcement of the Interest Equalization Tax (IET), enacted in 1964, which increased the effective cost of borrowing in the United States to most overseas borrowers. In 1965 a voluntary programme to limit banking flows and direct investment overseas was put into operation; at the beginning of 1968 these restraints were transformed into mandatory controls. The intention of these measures was primarily to shift the financing of United States overseas investment to foreign capital markets; they encouraged heavy borrowing by U.S. corporations in the Euro-bond and Euro-currency markets. An important purpose in the design of the reserve requirement against Euro-dollar borrowing by banks in 1968–1970 was to weaken the linkage between changes in U.S. domestic monetary conditions and the developments of the Euro-dollar market; banks were discouraged from repaying such debts by the provision that they would then lose part of the base from which future increases in borrowing were calculated. Though not unimportant in their total impact, these measures were swamped by the sharp fluctuations in short-term capital flows since about 1967. One of the aims of the changes in the dollar exchange rate since 1971 was to remove the need for more permanent capital controls. It became possible to take such steps after the large improvement on current account in 1973; in January 1974, the authorities announced the total removal of the IET and any other measures to stem capital outflows.

B.   THE DESIGN OF INSTRUMENT USE

The emphasis in the present section is on the targets of monetary policy. Ultimately the authorities aim to influence the major variables of the economy: the level of employment, the rate of change of aggregate demand and its major components, the rate of change of prices and the external balance. But without some readily observable variables which convey to the authorities information in summary form about on the one hand the impact of policy actions and on the other hand the course of ultimate target variables (for example, the state of demand in the economy), it is not possible in the short run for the authorities to assess reliably how monetary policy is affecting demand and what the "appropriate" stance of policy is in achieving these ultimate targets. For this purpose procedures have been developed for analysing these issues in terms of selected financial variables, so-called targets and indicators of monetary policy. Since these variables are more or less imperfect short cuts, it is not surprising that they have to be kept under constant and critical review and that they differ among countries in the light of the specific features of the financial system in question. It is the purpose of this section to bring out some main differences in approach. A technical note on criteria for selecting an optimal target for monetary policy will be found in the Annex.

A distinction is often made between operating and intermediate targets of monetary policy. *Operating targets* are those variables which are close to the classical instruments of monetary policy and may be regarded as potentially under control even over fairly short periods. Typical examples are short-term money market interest rates, net free reserves of the banking system and the monetary base. Information about them is available to the authorities with minimal delay, though some estimation is often involved on a day-to-day or week-to-week basis. The monetary authorities at any time know what the relevant short-term interest rates are, say in the markets for interbank funds or Treasury bills, and it is in their power, should they wish to exercise it, to push these rates to a desired level through open market operations or by other means. *Intermediate targets* are further remote from policy influences, though they may still be policy-dominated in the longer run. Examples are the broader monetary aggregates – relevant measures of the money stock and bank credit – and interest rates in markets where the authorities do not intervene directly or play a limited role, usually markets for longer-term securities. The classification of any particular financial target as operating or intermediate depends on the type of instruments relied on; in countries where ceilings on bank credit have been employed, this monetary aggregate may appropriately be regarded as an operating target. Most of the remaining discussion will be concerned with what are usually labelled operating targets, i.e. the monetary base and selected components thereof and short-term interest rates.

In reviewing the approach followed in the six countries, it may be useful to start from the common framework of a table showing the sources and uses of the monetary base (or, synonymously, reserve money or primary money). During any period – and neglecting discrepancies in accounting, mainly in the form of float – the following identity holds:

(1) Balance of payments surplus (+) or déficit (–) on official settlements;
+ (2) Government borrowing requirement;
– (3) New issues of government debt to domestic private sector;
+ (4) Net open market purchases;
+ (5) Increase in central bank lending;
= (6) Increase in non-bank holdings of currency;
+ (7) Increase in required reserves;
+ (8) Increase in excess reserves.

The official statistics published by the central banks in countries other than the United Kingdom contain a particular variant of this general framework; though the precise definitions used for some of the components differ, the individual structures are obtained by modest rearrangements of the above eight components.[1]

It is a crucial first step to distinguish, among the eight components, those that are *i*) instruments of policy, *ii*) exogenous, i.e. unrelated to monetary policy actions in the short run, and *iii*) endogenous, i.e. dependent on changes in instruments. In the first category are the three general policy instruments described in section *A* above, i.e. open market operations, changes in central bank lending and variations in reserve requirement ratios. However, as has already been pointed out above (pages 29 and 30), it may not be legitimate to regard all three of these as freely available to the authorities; if two of them are used actively in one direction, the third may have to act as a safety valve, giving way in the other direction. The components which the monetary authorities must regard as largely exogenous in the short run are (2), (3), (6) and a major part of (1). The Government borrowing requirement is planned by the Treasury or Ministry of Finance, while the influence of the central bank on the composition of the debt may be more significant. In some countries, most clearly the United States, (2) and (3) offset each other closely in their impact on liquidity, since any budgetary imbalance finds its way into a change in Government debt outstanding (except for fluctuations in working balances with commercial banks). Indeed, with the exception of Italy and France and to a minor extent Germany, the scope for any major net impact on the monetary base from items (2) and (3) combined appears limited, at least on an annual basis.[2] It remains, however, an important task of the central bank to project the major items of the central government budget and the financing of any imbalance, since this is a major influence on the course of interest rates and also since seasonal imbalances in government accounts can have a destabilizing impact on the monetary base in the shorter run.

Two further items are approximately independent of current monetary policy actions. The arguments are the clearest for currency demand: though large shifts in interest rates on assets which are substitutes for currency could be envisaged to affect non-bank holdings of currency, movements in such holdings are, in the short run, dominated by changes in aggregate

1. For the basic presentations of the five central banks see:
USA: Federal Reserve Bulletin, "Member Bank Reserves, Federal Reserve Bank Credit and Related Items" (Table A4).
Germany: Monatsberichte der Deutschen Bundesbank, "Zur Entwicklung der Bankenliquidität"; since March 1974, "Zentralbankgeldschafftung und freie Liquiditätsreverven der Banken" (Bankstatistische Gesamtrechnungen Tabelle 3).
France: Bulletin Trimestriel de la Banque de France, "Situation hebdomadaire de la Banque de France".
Italy: Banca d'Italia, Relazione Annuale, "Creazione e utilizzata del base monetario".
Japan: Bank of Japan Economic Statistics, "Factors of Changes in Bank Notes Issued" (Table 6) and "Accounts of the Bank of Japan" (Table 12).
See also, *United Kingdom: Bank of England Quarterly Bulletin*, "Influences on Money Stock and Domestic Credit Expansion", (Table 12/3). It should be noted that this table shows the sources of the money stock and domestic credit expansion, i.e. it includes lending by private financial institutions (see page 63).
2. In an extension of his earlier work on the measurement of fiscal policy to combined fiscal and monetary policy, Bent Hansen distinguishes between an American and a European type of "financing constraint". See "On the Effects of Fiscal and Monetary Policy; A Taxonomic Discussion"; *American Economic Review*, September 1973. An American type of constraint is the practice of financing any deficit or surplus on central government account by changes in outstanding debt; under a European type of constraint, such imbalances are reflected in changes of the monetary base.

demand which, in turn, must be assumed to be independent of current, though not past, monetary policy actions. Indeed, observing currency may be one of the better procedures for indirect assessment of major components of demand and income. A more complicated case is represented by the external position. As far as the current balance and most long-term capital movements are concerned, there can be little doubt about their exogeneity in the sense here used. But short-term private capital flows can obviously not be regarded as independent of current monetary policy actions, and particular attention must accordingly be devoted to analysing the probable response of capital flows to various policy actions.[1]

The final item of the list on page 51 is bank excess reserves. Regarded as a residual, this variable expresses the net effect of instruments and exogenous and endogenous influences. The authorities can choose this variable as an operating target, provided i) the banking system desires to hold a certain amount of excess reserves as a safety valve, and ii) the authorities have adequate information and the ability to forecast the other sources and uses of the monetary base. In rough terms these conditions have been met in the United States and Italy. In the other four countries excess reserves in the form of balances at the central bank have, throughout the period under study, been very small, virtually ruling out the possibility of using this variable as an operating target. In Germany, however, an extended concept of excess reserves, including also the borrowing potential at the Bundesbank has been used as an operating target (pages 58-60). It is therefore necessary to turn to the method of analysis and choice of operating target in the six countries. The following paragraphs will review how the design of instrument use in individual countries has been related to the possible targets in the basic identity of sources and uses of reserve money and the supplementary roles played by interest rates and monetary aggregates as targets of monetary policy.

Discussions of these issues have been most intensive in the *United States*.[2] In some respects the situation faced by the Federal Reserve has been simpler than in other countries: the exogenous elements among the sources and uses of monetary base have been relatively small with rather limited monetary effects from the central governments accounts and — until 1971 — modest-sized net impacts from the external sector (Chart 11). Both the huge size of the U.S. money market relative to even sizeable external imbalances and the position of the dollar as a reserve currency contributed to making the external impact quite manageable. Thus there has been comparatively little to predict and offset from these sources, leaving open market operations as the main source of the monetary base and shifts in the demand from banks as the major uncertain element in the interpretation of observed developments. During the period 1960–66, policy targets were formulated exclusively in terms of "money market conditions". The main

1. A further problem is whether the net foreign position of the banks is considered part of the use of the monetary base; if so, the appropriate definition of the external component of the sources is one that excludes movements of bank funds, i.e. the balance on non-monetary transactions rather than an official-settlements concept. This introduces an additional endogenous element into the basic identity unless the banks' net foreign position has been controlled administratively as was the case at times in Japan and Italy (pages 48-49).

2. OECD Monetary Studies Series, *Monetary Policy in the United States*, Appendix II. Much of the analysis carried out in recent years inside the Federal Reserve System may be found in *Open Market Policies and Operating Procedures*, Staff Studies, Board of Governors of the Federal Reserve System, Washington D.C., 1971.

elements in this concept were net free reserves of member banks and two interest rates, the interbank Federal funds rate and the Treasury bill rate; but these variables were seen as representatives of a larger group of financial variables. Net free reserves were measured as excess reserves minus borrowing, i.e. the difference between the stock concepts corresponding to items (8) and (5). Since net free reserves are not always related to the two interest rate variables in a stable and thus predictable way, the Federal Open Market Committee (FOMC) formulated free reserve targets in terms of ranges rather than single numbers, so that careful interpretation of policy directives was required in implementing its decisions. As a result of these experiences and the ongoing review of Federal Reserve procedures by the staff (encouraged also by criticism from academic economists of the emphasis on money market conditions) the main elements of an analysis for choosing an optimal target have emerged (see the Annex). At the same time, the formulation of policy targets has gradually widened.

Chart 11. SOURCES AND USES OF RESERVE MONEY: UNITED STATES
Quarterly changes

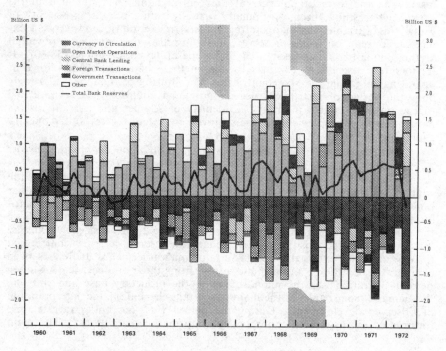

Three main stages in this process may be distinguished:
  i) *1966–69* when the so-called proviso clause entered into the directives of the FOMC;
  ii) *1970–71* when the monetary aggregates were given major emphasis; and
  iii) the *post-1971* phase in which experimentation has proceeded inside an aggregate-based strategy with new formulations of money market conditions, centering on a refined concept of reserves.

The proviso clause stipulated that the instructions relating to money market conditions would apply only if the growth rate of selected monetary aggregates did not deviate strongly from projections. But since the FOMC was eclectic in its choice of monetary aggregates — bank credit and the narrow and broad definitions of the money stock (M1 and M2) were all used — and did not specify narrow limits for tolerable deviations from projections, the proviso clause appears to have had limited operational significance in the 1966-69 phase. The aggregates were primarily used, in these years, not as policy targets, but as "variables for testing the consistency between money market conditions and projected developments in the real economy."[1]

Since 1970 the monetary aggregates have assumed greater though by no means exclusive importance. On a number of occasions they were referred to first in the directive, before any mention of money market conditions. Though the instructions of the FOMC are meant to be operational for the approximately four-week interval between meetings, there was no illusion, given the indirect methods available for influencing the aggregate, that bank credit and the money stock could be made to conform closely within such an interval to a prescribed course. In describing its own targeted growth rates for the aggregates, the FOMC referred to "the months ahead", usually interpreted to mean 3 to 6 months. Observed growth rates of the money stock tended to become more volatile in 1971 and at times clearly at variance with the intentions (projections) expressed in the directives, while the average growth rate for the year as a whole — 6 per cent — appears to have corresponded rather well with intentions. Though research tended to show that deviations from a targeted growth path for the money stock may have only very limited consequences, if they persist for no more than one or two quarters and are subsequently "compensated" by deviations in the opposite direction, the 1971 experiences prompted a further review of operating procedures in early 1972. While the aggregates, and particularly M1 and M2, continue to receive emphasis, the FOMC has begun to formulate target ranges for the growth in reserves against private deposits (RPD, measured as total member bank reserves minus those required to support Federal government and interbank deposits). Ranges of about 4 percentage points have been set for the targeted growth of RPD over two-month periods. While it has generally proved possible to keep RPD inside the targeted range, opinions about its reliability in keeping the monetary aggregates on course continue to differ. On the whole, RPD has hardly been used with single-mindedness to achieve a particular rate of growth of M1 or M2.[2] Indeed, in January 1974, the FOMC decided to publish numerical specifications also for the two measures of the money stock (M1 and M2) and the Federal funds rate. As in the case of RPDs, targets for M1 and M2 are expressed as ranges of tolerance over a 2-month period; that for the Federal funds rate is specified as a range for weekly average levels until the next meeting of the FOMC. It is recognized that not only bank reserves but also short-term interest rates such as the Federal funds rate should be changed gradually within their tolerated ranges, given the short-run volatility of the monetary aggregates and the possibility that abrupt

1. Axilrod S. H., in *Open Market Policies and Operating Procedures — Staff Studies.* Federal Reserve Board, July 1971, p. 20.
2. For an interpretation along these lines, see the annual reviews of open market policy in *Federal Reserve Bulletin* 1973 and 1974; see further A. Burger, "Money Stock Control, An Aggregate Approach", *unpublished* paper prepared for Konstanz Seminar, June 1974.

changes in the aggregates may later prove to be self-correcting. Depending on circumstances, the FOMC will widen or narrow the ranges of tolerance for the four numerically specified targets, and will vary the relative importance of each target.

To summarize the design of instrument use in the United States, the reserve money concept used has evolved from net free reserves (the difference between items (8) and (5) in the basic sources and uses table) towards a more aggregate concept, particularly RPD (which is the sum of (7) and (8) with various technical adjustments). At all times, short-term interest rates have been important additional targets; the monetary aggregates have come gradually to the fore as additional targets over the slightly longer run from the late 1960s. No targets have been announced for long-term interest rates; while those rates are thought to be very important in the transmission mechanism (pages 79 and 80), the influence of policy instruments is too remote and too lagged for these rates to be realistic policy targets over the horizon relevant in FOMC policy-making.

In *Italy*, the main policy target since about the mid-1960s has been the monetary base, i.e. the right-hand side of the basic identity on page 51; prior to 1965 excess reserves performed this role.[1] Among the sources of the monetary base, both the government accounts and the external balance have over long periods yielded important positive contributions, leaving only a limited need for strong expansionary actions through central bank credit (Chart 12). But this situation has been modified in recent years by the emergence of large and volatile outflows of capital, a deteriorating current account and growing government deficits; generally it has become more difficult to predict the exogenous sources and take appropriate offsetting measures. These developments have tended to erode the importance of the monetary base as a target.[2] There are some features specific to the Italian definition of the monetary base: it comprises the public's deposits with the postal system — though these deposits appear to be closer substitutes for bank deposits than of currency — and Treasury bills redeemable on demand; furthermore that part of the banks' net foreign exchange assets which may be freely repatriated and converted into lire according to prevailing Bank of Italy directives was included in excess reserves up to 1972. The transition from excess reserves to the monetary base was made because the monetary aggregates and notably bank credit, which throughout the period under review constituted an important additional target, were thought to be more easily predictable from the base than from the small and volatile figures for excess reserves. Since large shifts both in monetary policy actions and in other main sources of the monetary base tend to be reflected in excess reserves, the practical difference may not be very great. In analysis of the impact of monetary changes the Bank of Italy continues to disaggregate changes in the monetary base not only by use but also by source.

Targets for the monetary base are formulated only on an annual basis. The main purpose of the rounds of discussion and revisions which precede publication of a target is to provide a consistent framework for longer-run evaluation and not to guide policy operators in any efforts of short-run monetary management; targeted growth rates for the base have been watched as rough bench-marks for actual developments within the year.

1. OECD Monetary Studies Series, *Monetary Policy in Italy*, pp. 25-32.
2. Bank of Italy, Annual Report, 1973.

Chart 12. SOURCES AND USES OF RESERVE MONEY: ITALY
Quarterly changes

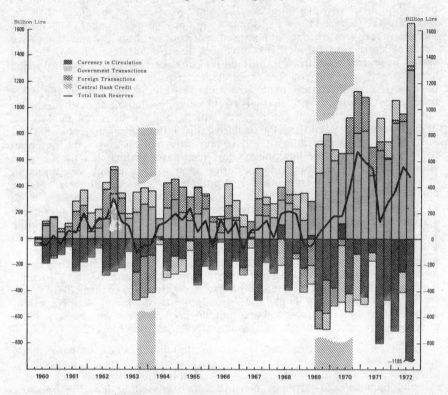

While they have not turned out to be further off the mark than in countries which have instituted procedures for "fine tuning" in monetary
management, this does raise the question of whether the Italian authorities
rely on shorter-term targets in addition to the longer-term ones for the
monetary base and bank credit. This was clearly the case in the 1966–69
period when the Bank of Italy pegged the interest rate in the market for long-
term government bonds and thereby indirectly rates in other securities
markets as well. Most of the three-year period was marked by a high
degree of financial stability, and pegging did not require large-scale open
market operations. After 1969 the monetary authorities intervened more
actively, mostly absorbing substantial volumes of bonds in order to limit
the rise in interest rates. The heavy outflows of non-bank capital forced
the authorities to accept some rise in rates and to find ways of limiting
the sensitivity of capital flows to shifts in relative monetary conditions. It
is not clear whether in Italian conditions an interest rate target is superior
to a "quantity" target – either in terms of the monetary base or bank
credit – in keeping a check on the external balance, and the Italian authorities are therefore adopting a pragmatic attitude. In 1973 they reinforced
their grip on this problem by active management of the terms of central
bank credit, and thereby indirectly deposit and lending rates, and by introducing ceilings on major categories of bank lending, while the monetary
base continues to provide the framework for longer-term consistency with
domestic aims.

In *Germany,* the preferred policy target has been "bank liquidity" or the ratio of this variable to deposits.[1] Prior to mid-1973 the volume of bank liquidity was measured as the sum of *i*) excess balances with the Bundesbank (Chart 13), *ii*) domestic money market paper, *iii*) money market investment abroad, *iv*) unused rediscount quotas and, as a negative item, *v*) short-term Bundesbank advances against collateral. This definition varied in several ways from traditional measures of reserves: it corresponded most closely to net free reserves, since required reserves and reserves borrowed through central bank advances were deducted, but on the other hand gross foreign money market assets were included along with domestic money market paper and the reserves which could be acquired by full use of rediscounting facilities. Particularly this latter item suggests that the purpose of the definition was to convey information about the potential lending capacity of the banking system. The reasons which led the German authorities to adopt this wide definition of a reserve target were inherent in the way the main monetary instruments were used. Monthly average balances with the Bundesbank in excess of requirements were kept close to zero as banks had every inducement in the availability of alternative assets which were liquid, but interest-bearing and safe, and in the flexible way in which the reserve requirements were set up to minimize such balances.[2] As noted above, the main policy instruments were changes in rediscount quotas and in reserve requirements, and it seemed convenient to use a policy target which illustrated the impact of both of these factors. An important longer-term target having been the rate of growth of bank credit, the usefulness of bank liquidity as a short-run target depends essentially on whether it provides more reliable predictions about bank lending in subsequent periods than a traditional reserve measure (page 74).

In its analysis of the sources of bank liquidity, the Bundesbank made use of a distinction between policy and market factors in the basic identity, whether exogenous or endogenous.[3] The dominant market factors were the external balance and currency demand which tended to move in opposite directions, since the external source (which prior to 1973 comprised not only the increase in the net foreign assets of the Bundesbank, but also gross changes in the banks' foreign assets) was on the average positive, though at the same time highly volatile. Government transactions were also at times an important factor, usually absorbing bank liquidity. It is against this background that the German monetary authorities designed the use of their main instruments, changes in rediscount quotas and in reserve requirements, to bring bank liquidity to the desired level consistent with the scope for increases in bank lending over a coming period. The introduction of restraint, as conceived by the Bundesbank, was on all four occasions characterized by a decline in the bank liquidity ratio, and its removal by a rise.[4]

In recent years, the usefulness of the concept of bank liquidity was subjected to increasingly severe criticism on its own logic, quite apart from

1. OECD Monetary Studies Series, *Monetary Policy in Germany,* pp. 39-42.
2. Chart 13 shows the difference between the level of banks' excess reserves at current and preceding end-quarters; their end-quarter level is calculated as the end-quarter level of banks' total reserves minus the daily average of required reserves.
3. This distinction is retained in the presentation of sources of bank liquidity in particular policy phases in the OECD Monetary Studies Series. See *Monetary Policy in Germany,* Charts 12-16.
4. *Ibid.,* Chart 11, p. 45.

Chart 13. SOURCES AND USES OF RESERVE MONEY: GERMANY
Quarterly changes

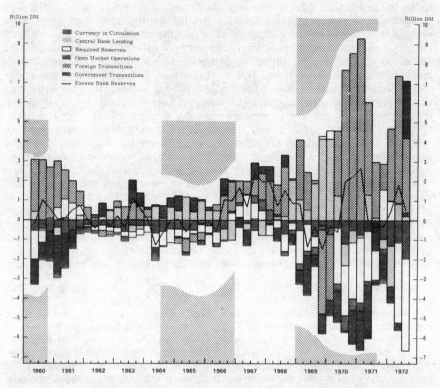

the difficulties in predicting bank behaviour from it. From 1970 the distinction between use of rediscount quotas and advances (Lombard credit) became increasingly blurred as Lombard credits approached a high degree of automaticity, thereby weakening the major reason for treating the two kinds of borrowing separately. Furthermore, during periods when the Deutschemark was floating, notably May-December 1971 and again from February 1973, it was not realistic to lump foreign money market assets with domestic ones. In June 1973 the Bundesbank has accordingly modified the definition of bank liquidity[1] to comprise only three items: *i*) excess balances at the Bundesbank, *ii*) domestic money market assets, *iii*) unused rediscounting within the rediscount quotas or the usable part of the quotas, and unused scope for Lombard credit within the "warning mark" prior to its suspension (page 36). Measured in per cent of total deposits − a ratio presentation is natural to facilitate comparison over time − the new definition was over the preceding three years 8 to 10 percentage points lower than the one previously used. On the new definition bank liquidity has moved in a range much closer to zero since March 1973.

In March 1974, the traditional analysis of bank liquidity by use and source was abandoned. Instead, a new table was introduced which shows the sum of *i*) the change in central bank money (defined as currency in circulation plus required reserves against domestic liabilities) and *ii*) the

1. *Monatsberichte der Deutschen Bundesbank*, June 1973.

change in bank liquidity, as well as determinants of the total change.[1] The Bundesbank's intention is not to use the sum total as a target of monetary policy or as an indicator in assessing the thrust of monetary policy. The first component, which represents item(6) in the identity shown on page 51, is determined mainly by the current level of income and is thus removed from current policy actions, although large changes in interest rates on substitutes for currency can slightly influence demand. The second component, which corresponds to most of item (7) in that identity, is included only to establish arithmetical relationships with the determining factors. As this represents the scope for potential central bank money creation, its level is also shown separately. But since it was reduced virtually to zero, changes in the availability of central bank money, through which the Bundesbank aims to influence banks' lending attitudes, cannot, of course, be assessed by the observation of bank liquidity. In the new situation where the central bank controls the supply of central credit even on a day-to-day basis, such short-term interest rates as inter-bank rates, which closely reflect the demand and supply relationships for bank reserves, should represent the short-run thrust of monetary policy more accurately than prior to 1973. Then, the management of bank liquidity was conducted in principle on a monthly basis, and some element of endogeneity was left in the shorter-run fluctuations in these interest rates, although a fairly close negative relationship was observed between their monthly changes and the development of bank liquidity.

In *Japan* the main target of monetary policy has been bank credit to the private non-financial sectors.[2] For most of the period up to 1970–71, this was virtually the same as a money supply target, since the impact from the external sector was small and rather well controlled through the extensive regulations pertaining to capital flows and also because bank credit to the public sector was relatively unimportant. Bank reserves have been maintained very close to required minimum levels, while the demand for currency has been growing rapidly along with the rise in money incomes. As for sources of the monetary base, the main policy factor was Bank of Japan lending; not only the external account but also the government's net cash transactions exerted a limited influence and securities operations were never undertaken on any large scale, though they did come increasingly into use for short-run adjustment in recent years (Chart 14). In phases of monetary restraint the rise in Bank of Japan credits available lagged, though in retrospect only slightly, behind the pace at which the currency drain reduced reserves. The result was a very sharp rise in call-money (inter-bank) rates in the first two phases of restraint and a more modest rise in later phases when the degree of domestic restraint aimed at was less severe. There is nothing to suggest, however, that call-money rates were themselves seen as a target. The indirect control over bank credit expansion was supplemented by applying ceilings for credit expansion initially to the city banks, and subsequently to a wider range of financial institutions. These ceilings during restrictive periods as well as the system of "liquidity position guidance" which replaced it between October 1969 and end-1970 underline that the thinking of the Japanese authorities was focused on bank credit as the dominant target. Since 1971 when the balance of payments surplus considerably reinforced the monetary effect of domestic credit expansion, fuller account of the external monetary impact has been taken in designing

1. *Ibid.*, July 1974.
2. OECD Monetary Studies Series, *Monetary Policy in Japan*, pp. 29-31.

the use of policy instruments geared to the control of domestic bank lending, although no specific targets have been set for the money supply.

Chart 14. SOURCES AND USES OF RESERVE MONEY: JAPAN
Quarterly changes

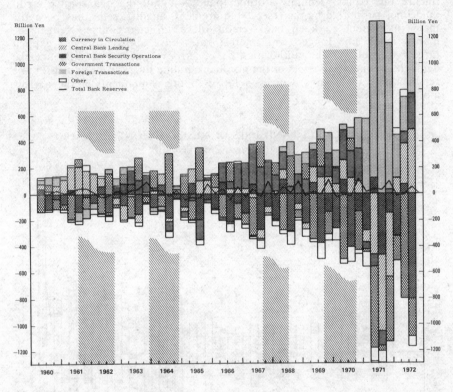

The situation in *France* has in important respects been similar to that in Japan: bank credit has been the dominant target and, in restricted periods, the authorities have relied on direct ceilings on bank lending, and more recently on reserve requirements against lending which has much the same effect (see page 41). But in contrast to Japan where ceilings were applied only to part of the banking system (deposit money banks) and the availability effect of central bank lending policy has been actively used to influence the course of total bank credit, the French authorities subjected all banks to quantitative controls; the rationing effect of central bank credit has not until recently been relied upon. As in Japan the banks have been operating at near zero levels of excess reserves and have been largely indebted to the central bank; but unlike in Japan the extension of central bank credit has been rather automatic until recently.[1] Prior to 1968, reliance on cost effects in influencing bank credit was also limited by the authorities' preference for low interest rates. Since that year the authorities have assumed a more flexible attitude to the formulation of interest rate policy,

1. OECD Monetary Studies Series, *Monetary Policy in France*, Part III.B.

but its use to influence bank credit (by varying the cost of central bank credit and by pushing the banks to make heavier use of such credit through increases in reserve requirements) has been constrained in more recent years by the increased interest sensitivity of international capital. In 1973, the authorities started to restrain the availability of central bank credit to influence the banks' lending attitude (page 28), but the quantitative credit guideline, supported by the reserve requirements against credit, has been the main instrument to keep bank credit on a targeted course. Neither the money stock nor longer-term interest rates have apparently been explicit targets of policy. The authorities have, however, aimed to influence the demand for financial assets of the non-bank public by assuring a rise in the remuneration of savings deposits relative to the components of the narrow money supply.

Chart 15.   SOURCES AND USES OF RESERVE MONEY: FRANCE
Quarterly changes

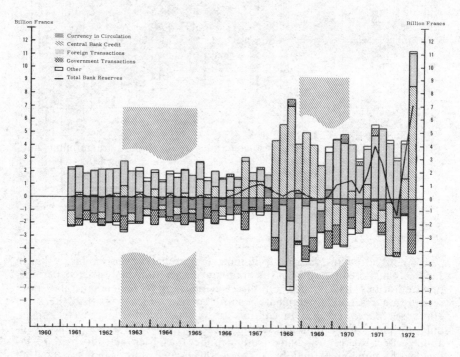

The case of the *United Kingdom* is more complicated to interpret, particularly since the design of instrument use has apparently changed more drastically during the last decade than anywhere else, not excluding the United States. Three phases may be distinguished: *i*) pre-1968–69, *ii*) 1969–1971 and *iii*) the period following the introduction of *Competition and Credit Control* in 1971. During the first phase, the main policy target was bank credit, and quantitative targets were specified with increasing frequency from 1965 onwards as ceilings became a major instrument. There was no emphasis on a reserve target. Short-term interest rates were considered a target and were frequently allowed to vary substantially to influence capital flows. Long-term rates were targets only in the more structural sense of debt management policy (page 27). Thus, during this early phase bank credit and interest rates were viewed as targets designed to achieve different – and at times conflicting – objectives. In the second phase between late 1968 and 1971, broader monetary aggregates tended to become the dominant targets while open market operations became geared more closely to short-term monetary management. During the financial years 1969–1970 and 1970–71, explicit targets for domestic credit expansion (DCE) were set forth by the government as part of a comprehensive programme to establish external equilibrium. DCE was defined as the change in the broad money supply adjusted for the impact of external factors; the concept was integrated into the analysis of money demand and supply.

The reforms announced in the consultative document *Competition and Credit Control* in May 1971 marked a sharper break with the previous design of monetary policy. In particular, while it emphasized the monetary aggregates as targets (and with the money stock given more prominence), it abolished the direct method of controlling them through ceilings and replaced it by more indirect methods, mainly through the management of the volume of eligible reserve assets[1] and by indicating a readiness to use not only short-term, but also longer-term interest rates more actively; outright support operations by the Bank of England in the markets for maturities of more than one year were suspended. Following a period of adjusting to the new concept, a situation appears to have been established in which there is hardly any excess of eligible reserves. This does not signify, however, that the operation of United Kingdom monetary policy has become very similar to that in the United States where the scope for creating excess reserves through the actions of the banks are minimal and borrowing at the central bank severely circumscribed. The U.K. definition of eligible reserves includes some assets the availability of which is not unrelated to banks' demand for them, notably call loans (primarily to the discount houses). Though some of the scope for producing such assets was eliminated in 1973 the reserve concept seems to retain a greater endogenous element than in the other countries surveyed. This makes an analysis along the traditional lines of sources and uses of " eligible reserve money " less natural than in other countries; in fact no such analysis is presented in U.K. financial analysis which moves straight to a breakdown by sources and uses of the total money stock.[2]

Until very recently explicit targets for the growth rates of the monetary aggregates have not been formulated. This was due to the coincidence during 1971–73 of expansionary, or at least accommodating, policies and the general recognition by the authorities of the desirability of letting the banks recapture, through a phase of " reintermediation ", some of the relative decline experienced by the banks inside the financial sector during the long period of credit ceilings. Furthermore, the presence of some temporary factors, acting to inflate the rate of growth of broadly-defined money – M3, comprising also sterling certificates of deposit – made it hazardous to formulate policy in terms of at least M3. On the other hand, a narrower measure of money (M1) excluding longer-term deposits, appeared to be

1. See the definition in footnote 5 on page 39.
2. *Bank of England Quarterly Bulletin*, "Influences on Money Stock and Domestic Credit Expansion", Table 12/3.

rather more closely related to movements in current income through the demand for transactions balances, and it seemed to reflect only to a modest extent any short-term thrust of monetary policy. A further review of these experiences is made on page 81 below; here it may merely be noted that the initial intention of the U.K. authorities to rely on interest rate changes and variations in the volume of eligible reserve assets available — a selection of variables to characterize U.K. "money market conditions" — were modified by the December 1973 "supplementary scheme" based on increases in interest-earning liabilities. In view of the sharply progressive scale of penalties, and the fact that the banks have been told that they are not expected to pass on the higher cost of funds through increased interest charges to their customers, this instrument should effectively restrain the annual growth rate of the banks' interest-bearing liabilities — the most rapidly growing component of M3 in the period since 1971 — to about 17 per cent. It is significant that a quantitative target has been made public for the first time under the regime of *Competition and Credit Control*.

Having reviewed the practices of the six countries as they have evolved over the years since 1960, it may seem hazardous to attempt any summary. Not only have these practices differed between countries; they have also been modified in ways which show no obvious convergence. Yet in returning to the questions posed initially in the present discussion (page 53), some common conclusions do appear. As for the role of short-term interest rates as a target, it was not explicitly used in some countries (Japan, Italy); in some others where it was given much prominence at one time or another (United States, United Kingdom), it has tended to decline in importance relative to either a measure of reserves or the monetary aggregates. There has also been a tendency for administrative controls over interest rates to recede, the gradual shrinking of the applicability of Regulation Q in the United States being the main example. Bank credit has been, at times, an important target in all six countries; four of them have at times formulated targets for bank credit and applied ceilings to achieve them, and the two which have not (United States and Germany) have clearly had much more than vague notions about the appropriate course for bank credit. It has not always been obvious whether bank credit targets were conceived of as worthwhile in themselves or as a means of keeping the money stock on a desired course. In countries with efficient controls on capital flows and relatively limited current balances, the practical difference has often not been great (Japan, France). In others where capital flows have been relatively large (Germany, Italy, United Kingdom), the two targets may serve difference purposes, bank credit expansion being a more appropriate target to achieve external objectives and the money supply to achieve internal objectives. Finally, where the scope for disintermediation — and its reversal, reintermediation — is considerable (United States, United Kingdom), both bank credit and the money stock, particularly when broadly defined, may fluctuate rather sharply around a targeted growth rate without representing major departures from the intended thrust of policy. It is therefore understandable that the respective monetary authorities have been reluctant to commit their prestige to accurate attainment of any one particular target; the experiences in Germany, the United States and the United Kingdom underline major reasons why the central banks adopt an eclectic attitude in their endeavours to design an appropriate aggregate-based strategy for the use of their monetary instruments.

This review has shown important divergences among the six countries with respect to their choice of targets in the basic identity for sources and uses of reserve money. The main difference is between those that define a reserve target which leaves an endogenous element to be influenced substantially by bank behaviour or which is so vague as to constitute only a weak constraint on banks, and those which adopt a narrower concept, more closely dominated by policy instruments and other exogenous factors. The clearest example of the latter is the United States where borrowing facilities at the central bank are viewed as a privilege, not a right; banks cannot count on supplementing their excess reserves by borrowing except for very short-run purposes. When the supply of non-borrowed reserves − the net effect of items (1) to (4) and (6) in the basic identity − decelerates, only a limited part is typically offset by borrowing. The change therefore relatively quickly generates pressure on the banks to reduce their demand for reserves to match the reduction in supply; and the means for the banks to achieve this is by slowing down the pace at which they acquire earning assets. The process may be prolonged, but it is inescapable in a system where the banks have no short-cuts to supplement their reserves. In Japan also, the central bank uses changes in the availability of central bank lending as an important instrument to influence banks' lending attitudes.[1] It is interesting to note that the two countries referred to as examples operate at widely different levels of bank borrowing at the central bank; whereas borrowing is negligible in the United States it has typically constituted 40 per cent or more of the monetary base in Japan (Chart 8). What matters is not the level of borrowing by the banking system as a whole but the scope which individual banks believe they have for increasing it.

101. The situation has differed, in varying degrees, from this pattern in the four other countries either by including a wider range of assets − most of them interest-bearing − in the measurement of reserves (Germany, Italy, United Kingdom) or by allowing a greater degree of automaticity in central bank lending (until recently Germany, France). In all four cases, the impact of policy instruments and other exogenous sources of reserve money on the readiness of banks to extend credit is not easily measurable. Germany has had the arrangements with the most flexibility, and bank liquidity was apparently well above the level at which downward pressure could be expected to set in motion the type of adjustment process described above. Bank liquidity seemed to behave as a buffer among the banks' potential assets; even in periods of restraint the size of this buffer remained substantial. But in 1973, the Bundesbank fundamentally modified this situation by introducing measures to reduce bank liquidity to an unprecedently low level and tightening its grip on the supply of reserves. Similar though less dramatic steps have been reviewed in the case of the three other countries; France and Italy have changed banks' evaluation of central bank credit by making it available in a more discretionary and onerous way, steps which are bound to dampen the readiness of banks to run their excess reserves down to very low levels. The Bank of England has reduced the scope for banks to supplement their eligible reserve assets through transactions with the discount houses. These steps point to convergence in the thinking of the monetary authorities in the six countries.

1. For details see OECD Monetary Studies Series, *Monetary Policy in Japan*, p. 31.

III

IMPACT OF MONETARY POLICY
ON DOMESTIC FINANCIAL VARIABLES
AND EXTERNAL CAPITAL FLOWS

A.   IMPACT ON DOMESTIC FINANCIAL VARIABLES

The impact of monetary policy on the financial variables which are somewhat remote from the control of the authorities is a crucial link in the evaluation of policy. This section reviews the closeness of the link between the chosen policy target(s) and variables which indicate the actual thrust originating from the financial sector. As will be evident from the survey in Part IV, indicators of financial thrust found useful in the six countries include the rates of growth of various broader monetary aggregates, possibly supplemented by credit extended by specialized institutions, and interest rates. Thus a review will be made in the following paragraphs on the developments of these variables in the years 1960–1972. There are two important domestic factors which come to the fore in any comparative analysis of the efficiencies of monetary policies in influencing domestic financial variables. They are i) the ease with which lenders and borrowers can bypass the domestic banking system towards which most of the available instruments are directed, and ii) the degree of rigidity in interest rate formation. These factors are interrelated, competitive bidding for funds typically being associated with a domestic financial system where the transition from one market to another is relatively easy. The degree of accuracy with which the authorities can influence the course of domestic financial variables depends also in part on the degree of external openness of the financial economy. This section will therefore briefly touch upon the effects of external transactions on domestic monetary developments, leaving for Section B a more detailed analysis of the sensitivity of capital flows to changes in relative monetary conditions.

In reviewing the experiences of the six countries with respect to controlling domestic financial variables, it seems worthwhile to make an attempt to rank the six countries by the degree of segmentation and rigidity of their financial structure. Japan and France tend to have the most stable pattern of financial flows; non-bank sources of domestic funds, whether from depository institutions or securities markets, are either sufficiently controlled or unimportant relative to the banking system proper, so as to make bank lending a useful summary of the monetary thrust. The flexibility in interest rates and the scope for substitution appear to have been greater in Italy and Germany, though not nearly so great as in the United

67

Kingdom and the United States. The two Anglo-Saxon economies have offered the closest approximation to a competitive financial system with a minimum of administrative control over longer-term markets. The implications of such a system are not necessarily that monetary policy works more slowly or imprecisely than in a financial system characterized by many elements of rationing and rigidity. The implications are rather that it is not particularly useful in a flexible system to aim at precise targets for particular credit flows or even for (some relevant definition of) the money stock; interest rates may often give better guidance.

A major difficulty in assessing the appropriateness of observed interest rate developments has in recent years been associated with changing – i.e. mainly accelerating – inflationary expectations. Such expectations are only crudely portrayed by recently observed rates of change of selected prices indices. In normal circumstances, inflationary expectations may be assumed to respond only slowly to observed price trends so that one may infer from, say, the increase in nominal bond rates usually accompanying the introduction of monetary restraint that the real cost of capital has moved in the same direction. But there are episodes to which this assumption hardly applies; sharp and well-publicized accelerations of prices may well in recent years have triggered a lowering of the real cost of capital in restrictive phases when nominal rates were observed to rise.[1] In any case the importance of changes in inflationary expectations over longer periods makes it highly arbitrary to compare the severity of restraint between policy phases simply in terms of the respective levels of nominal rates. However, real interest rates are not easy to calculate. In the empirical work by the OECD Secretariat, reported in Part IV, a particularly simple formation of price expectations has been assumed; the observed rate of change in a relevant price series has simply been deducted from the nominal interest rate. (This type of variable was found to contribute significantly to the explanation of private investment in the cases of France and Germany). This is very much an *ad hoc* assumption, though it may still be easier to defend than the alternative of making no allowance for observed price changes so often used in the past in econometric models.

Turning to the experiences of individual countries, with respect to controlling domestic financial variables, *Japan* represents an extreme case of close control on broader monetary aggregates during the period under review. Lending by the major (city and long-term credit) banks has been so highly controlled by means of the rationing of central bank credit supplemented by ceilings that it is legitimate to regard this component of the aggregates as a direct policy instrument, at least in periods of monetary restraint.[2] It may be worth noting that the active use of this instrument did not make the growth rate of bank lending more volatile than in other economies; on the contrary, the growth rates of both major bank credit and of other monetary aggregates appear to have been smoother in Japan than in the other five countries surveyed (Chart 16). The introduction of monetary restraint coincided closely with a deceleration in major bank

1. The accelerating trend in prices since 1968–69 may have worked its way through to inflationary expectations with short time lags; nonetheless, even the sharp rise in nominal interest rates during the restrictive phase of 1973–74 does not seem to have pushed real rates to historically high levels. For an analysis along these lines, see *OECD Economic Outlook*, No. 14, December 1973.

2. OECD Monetary Studies Series, *Monetary Policy in Japan*, pp. 34 ff.

lending. In the second and third phases of restraint, deceleration even set in prior to the announced change in policy; the Bank of Japan had gradually begun to tighten its lending facilities prior to the official announcement. Subsequent relaxations led to a prompt acceleration of major bank lending with one important exception: in the reflationary period starting at the end of 1964, a pick-up got underway only in the latter half of 1966, because the demand for loans was very sluggish.

Chart 16. MONETARY AGGREGATES: JAPAN
Seasonally adjusted annual rate of change over previous quarter

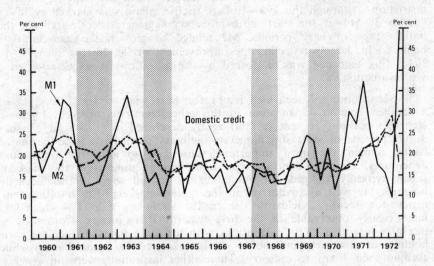

It is only lending by the major banks that has been under the immediate influence of monetary policy for most of the period under study. It is therefore more remarkable that also lending by other financial institutions has reflected rather closely the changing policy stance. Generally, these other institutions have been growing relatively faster than the major banks; this tendency does not appear to be related to their greater remoteness from the monetary authorities, since there is no evidence to suggest that their share in total lending grew faster in periods of monetary restraint. The parallel movement in lending by controlled and non-controlled institutions can be explained primarily by the dependence of the latters' loanable funds upon the proceeds of lending by major banks. However, in the two restrictive phases of the early 1960s, a sharp increase in money market rates also contributed to keep lending by the two groups in line, as the other financial institutions had a strong inducement to acquire money market assets in preference to direct lending — one of the comparatively rare exemples of relatively efficient control over a monetary aggregate by means of short-term rates.[1] As for the other two main sources of funds to offset loans from the major banks — issues of securities domestically

1. For econometric evidence, see OECD Monetary Studies Series, *Monetary Policy in Japan*, Appendix III, p. 93-97.

and borrowing abroad – both played a smaller role in Japan than in the other countries surveyed. As will be reviewed in the following section, the inflow of funds was screened carefully in the case of longer-term transactions and kept within rather narrow bounds for short-term non-monetary capital until 1971 when prepayments in dollars for Japanese exports swelled in response to expectations of a yen revaluation. Thus for most of the period under review, external effects on monetary expansion originated largely from changes in the Japanese current account position and tended to reinforce the effect of domestic credit expansion.[1] In the first three restrictive phases, for example, an external deficit tended to keep the growth rate of M2 below that of domestic credit in the initial months of restriction. Although the 1969–1970 restrictive phase was marked by faster growth of M2 at the start, both monetary aggregates decelerated. In the initial stage of easy periods, M2 tended to grow faster than domestic bank credit, largely reflecting the improvement of the current account. In 1971, this tendency was reinforced by capital inflows in expectation of a yen revaluation.

Substitution of securities issues for borrowing at banks has played a smaller role in Japan than in the other countries surveyed. Japanese securities markets are not yet sufficiently developed to absorb large issues during periods of increasing monetary tightness, particularly since the major banks remain the most important subscribers to industrial bonds and debentures. On the contrary, the tight lending policies of the Bank of Japan typically obliged the major banks to sell some of their security holdings (as well as to borrow in the money market). The resulting tendency for security yields to rise in the secondary market – which was most clearly observable in the first two restrictive phases – provided an incentive for other credit institutions with available funds to increase their holdings of securities (and money market loans to the major banks) while curbing their loans to industry. These other institutions were, in general, not ready to increase subscriptions for new issues of long-term bonds, as yields to new subscribers remained almost stable at fairly low levels even in tight money periods.[2] The relatively rigid yields on new issues and the limited importance of the securities market as a source of corporate funds support the view that the availability of bank credit has been the key financial variable influencing the course of private, and particularly business, expenditures. The institutional characteristics surveyed supply a rationale for regarding the rate of growth of bank credit as the main target for policy.

In *France*, reliance on ceilings on bank credit combined with the extensive controls on capital flows (pages 41 and 49) tended to produce results for the course of the monetary aggregates comparable to those in Japan.[3] In both the 1963–65 and the 1969–1970 restrictive phases bank credit decelerated; in the former phase in the course of the first six months of restraint, in the latter phase from the second half of 1969, when ceilings were tightened and the rate of growth of total domestic bank credit dropped

1. *Ibid.*, Chart 13, p. 45.
2. Insofar as these institutions purchase securities in the secondary market and the funds obtained by the selling banks are mopped up through the Bank of Japan's restrictive lending policy, there will, *ceteris paribus*, be no net increase in the total credits accorded by the financial system.
3. OECD Monetary Studies Series, *Monetary Policy in France*, Part IV.B.

sharply (Chart 17). Again in the third restrictive phase the growth of credit has been severely dampened by means of the recommendations by the Bank of France coupled with heavy sanctions in the form of reserve requirements against credit. Conversely, in periods of monetary ease, bank credit has accelerated following the removal of ceilings.

Chart 17. MONETARY AGGREGATES: FRANCE
Seasonally adjusted annual rate of change over previous quarter

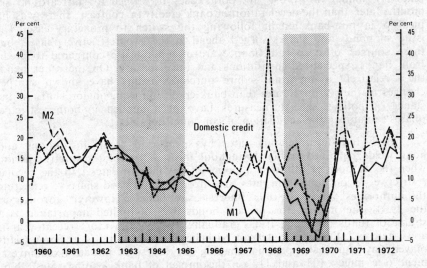

The course of the two other monetary aggregates, M1 and M2, has not differed widely from that of bank credit; both decelerated sharply in the two early phases of restraint. During the earlier of these phases the external imbalance was very small; in the second phase the improvement in the external position from the first months of 1970 pushed the growth rate of the money stock somewhat ahead of that of total bank credit. While it has not been the explicit aim of the authorities to establish a target for the money stock, attempts have been made to depress the growth rate of M1 in favour of longer-term deposits less directly related to future spending. In 1966–67 the interest differential in favour of such deposits widened sharply, as interest on sight deposits was suspended and administrative controls on time deposits rates were eased. Largely as a result of this shift, the growth rate of M1 fell sharply below that of M2 in the course of 1967. There is one further way in which the Bank of France has used interest rates to influence the course of the monetary aggregates. As pointed out above (page 33), variations in the cost of central bank credit were seen as an important indirect means of influencing the readiness of banks to extend their lending. This strategy was used in 1969 as a supplement to ceilings and to reinforce other measures against outflows of funds, but it is difficult to assess on the basis of available evidence whether the effects were significant beyond raising the cost of borrowing by the non-bank sectors.

71

While it must be concluded that the control of bank credit in France has been about as close as in Japan, the Treasury's direct credit and lending by special credit institutions under its control — none of which has been subject to ceilings — has provided a somewhat greater scope than in Japan for compensating financial adjustments through the central bank's control on bank credit. Thus, credits extended by specialized institutions and by the Treasury have followed a somewhat different pattern from that of bank credit. Although there was in both restrictive phases some deceleration of such credits, it was of short duration in 1963–64 and was relatively milder in 1969; in both cases it seemed to start around six months later than the deceleration in bank credit. In contrast, there was no pick-up in non-bank credit following the switch to monetary ease. The issue of bonds and shares surged ahead in the two restrictive phases, but these sources of corporate finance are of modest size compared to credit from banks, specialized institutions and the Treasury. On the other hand, the — relatively unimportant — hire purchase credits have shown sharper changes in their growth rates than bank credit following major shifts in the stance of policy; special measures have been applied in both restrictive phases to dampen the acquisition of consumer durables.

Both long-term lending rates by specialized credit institutions and bond yields remained stable throughout most of the first restrictive period when the authorities followed a policy of low interest rates.[1] In the second restrictive period, long-term rates rose more promptly and sharply, reflecting the authorities' more flexible interest rate policy. However, throughout the 1960s the market for private bonds was of limited importance as a source of funds (although it has gradually developed in more recent years); and there is little *a priori* reason to believe that variations in bond yields played any significant part in shaping the course of private fixed investment (see pages 103 and 112 on the impact of bank lending rates). Nor does the role of bond yields in allocating financial savings appear to have been important: while there is some evidence that a relative increase in longer-term deposit rates in 1966–67 seems to have prompted a shift towards "épargne liquide" the substitution between deposits and bonds seems much more limited.

In *Italy*, since the mid-1960s, the preferred operating target has been the monetary base, manipulation of which has clearly influenced the broader monetary aggregates (Chart 18).[2] All aggregates decelerated sharply around the introduction of monetary restraint in the third quarter of 1963; the movement was extremely sharp for both domestic credit and M1 which nearly stopped growing in the second half of 1964. In the 1969–1970 restrictive phase, the growth of the monetary base actually accelerated, restraint being characterized more by the upward shift in interest rates and some elements of rationing. But the growth rates of M1 and bank credit remained approximately stable while M2 decelerated reflecting the deterioration of the balance of payments. The relationship of the monetary base to banks' acquisition of earning assets (i.e. lumping together direct lending and purchases of bonds) appeared to be relatively stable, though subject to rather long time lags in the period up to around

1. A noticeable rise in early 1965 was the result of a tax measure and did not represent a change in interest rate policy.
2. OECD Monetary Studies Series, *Monetary Policy in Italy*, Charts 3 and 4, pp. 31-32 and pp. 44 ff.

1970.[1] The main finding in empirical work at the Bank of Italy has been that the direct effect of an increase in the supply of non-borrowed reserves, *ceteris paribus*, is to allow for an increase in bank lending and security holdings approximately seven times as large, spread rather evenly over a period of 5 to 6 quarters.[2] The credit multiplier has shifted upwards as a result of the lowering of effective reserve requirements in 1965; prior to then it was around four. The length of the time lags involved provides a rationale for the reluctance of the Bank of Italy to formulate precise shorter-term targets in terms of the monetary base; to justify such targets in terms of their supply effects would require accurate forecasting of the course of the real economy one year or more ahead.

Chart 18. MONETARY AGGREGATES: ITALY
Seasonally adjusted annual rate of change over previous quarter

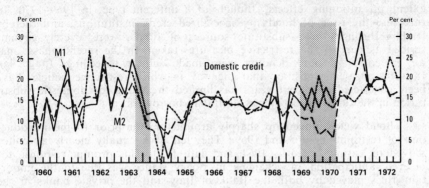

The above analysis has proceeded on the assumption that other factors, including interest rates, remain constant. When the supply of the monetary base decelerates, say in the case of a mounting external deficit, interest rates are likely to rise, an effect which is reinforced by smaller bank purchases (or even sales) of securities. Since banks' demand for reserves is significantly influenced by the rates they can earn on loans and securities, the tendency for rates to rise will depress the demand for reserves, thereby tending to offset the initial contractionary impact of the deceleration in the monetary base. What is observed in reality is a mixed supply-demand response in financial markets. With credit supply tending to be more elastic than demand, the credit multiplier effects suggested by the analysis above are substantially dampened, possibly to little more than one fourth. Thus, with sufficiently flexible changes in interest rates to establish a new equilibrium in the market, the credit multiplier is reduced to about two.[3] It may be that this way of viewing adjustments in financial

1. See particularly G. Caliguiri, A. Fazio, T. Padoa-Schioppa, "Demand and Supply of Bank Credit in Italy", *Journal of Money, Credit and Banking*, November 1974, pp. 455–479.

2. Reserves borrowed at the central bank may also form the basis for a credit expansion; the calculations assume, however, that there is no multiplying effect on credit supply in this case. For a criticism of this view, see OECD, Monetary Studies Series, *Monetary Policy in Italy*, p. 45, n. 2.

3. *Ibid.*, Technical Note to Part III, pp. 51–52.

markets exaggerates the degree of substitution in the Italian financial sector; the aggregation of credit flows through banks and the bond market would seem to imply a higher degree of perfection in the financial sector than the apparent rigidity of bank lending and deposit rates and the institutional structure in general would suggest. It would imply in particular that interest rates nay be more important than credit availability in transmitting the effects f monetary policy, contrary to the impression created by official statements on policy during restrictive phases.

It is important, therefore, to supplement the equilibrium analysis of credit markets with other work which allows for the possibility of disequilibrium and rationing elements. Some evidence of an increasing degree of rationing may be found in 1970, particularly in the size composition of bank loans; a decline of the share of small-size loans was clearly observable. It is also beyond doubt that the authorities themselves relied to some extent on rationing effects, though of a different type, in 1969–1970. In this case the issue of bonds by specialized credit institutions, and thereby lending through these substitute sources of funds, were severely circumscribed as part of the restrictive measures taken. In the recent phase, major categories of bank lending were made subject to ceilings (page 43). It seems a safe proposition that the way in which restrictive policies have been conducted in recent years has limited the scope for domestic substitution in the funds raised by private Italian borrowers.

Bond yields moved up sharply around or even prior to the introduction of restraint in 1963 and 1969.[1] They fell back equally clearly as policy moved to easing in early 1964 and late 1970. This prompt response to, or even anticipation of, changes in policy stance was due to the important roles played by both the Bank of Italy and the private banks in the market for government securities (page 28). During the tightening of monetary policy in 1973 the increase in bond rates became sharper than desired for domestic purposes; the authorities effectively checked the tendency for banks to let restraint be reflected primarily in declining purchases of bonds by imposing ceilings on direct lending combined with minimum holdings of bonds. These measures made it possible to twist the relationship between the cost of borrowing in the bond and bank loan markets as the discount rate was increased. These experiences and the long phase of pegging in 1966–69 demonstrate that the policy impact on long-term rates is potentially very important even within relatively short periods of time; but the end of pegging in 1969 points to the limitations on the power of the authorities to hold on to a level of rates considered appropriate on domestic grounds in the face of rising rates abroad.

In *Germany*, the pace of expansion of domestic bank credit (chart 19) showed some responsiveness to movements in the preferred policy target, the bank liquidity ratio.[2] In the 1959–1960 restrictive phase, there was a particularly sharp deceleration; it was followed by a strong recovery from late 1960 when policy was eased. In the second restrictive phase, the deceleration was more gentle and the lag behind the turning point of the liquidity ratio as long as nearly one year. In 1969–1971 the relationship between the two was not obvious: while the liquidity ratio declined quite sharply in most of 1969, bank credit did not decelerate significantly; and

1. OECD Monetary Studies Series, *Monetary Policy in Italy*, pp. 35-44.
2. OECD Monetary Studies Series, *Monetary Policy in Germany*, Chart 11.

from late 1970 bank credit accelerated steadily despite a low, declining ratio. Generally bank customers can draw in a quasi-automatic manner on previously arranged credit lines, and, in practice, there has proved to be scope for large changes in their utilization. Thus changes in pressures on bank liquidity have shown up mainly in fluctuations in banks' purchases of bonds, though the year 1971 was, also in this respect, a departure from earlier experiences in that banks continued to acquire bonds despite their strained liquidity.

Chart 19. MONETARY AGGREGATES: GERMANY
Seasonally adjusted annual rate of change over previous quarter

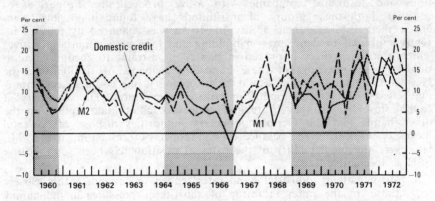

Closer examination of the timing pattern of the growth rates of two measures of the money stock in relation to turning points in the bank liquidity ratio does not bring out any close relationship, though the link is firmer than that of bank credit to the ratio. The narrow money supply (M1) behaved in an approximately anti-cyclical way in the first two phases of restraint. But throughout 1970 and in the first half of 1971, while the liquidity ratio moved more gently upwards, M1 accelerated very sharply. To some extent the looseness of the relationship between timing patterns in the two series may be attributed to the differential impact of external influences on bank liquidity and the money stock. For example, an inflow (which initially boosts the two by the same absolute amount) will increase the ratio since liquidity is by far the smaller of the two; over some period thereafter, both banks and non-banks adjust to longer-term portfolio equilibria, and the liquidity ratio will be declining as the rate of bank credit expansion accelerates (or possibly remains stable). A further factor which has destabilized the link from the ratio to M1 is the apparently high degree of substitution between M1 and the longer-term deposits which make up M2 together with it. In particular, since 1967 when bank deposit rates were liberalized, there has been active arbitrage among deposits of different maturities, and accelerations of demand and time deposits have accordingly at times been inversely related. This is an argument in favour of using the broad money stock (M2) as the main indicator of monetary thrust. The main divergences were in the years 1966–1968 when the spread between longer and shorter-term rates tended to widen. Another factor was the slack in the German economy during much

75

of this period, which tended to shift the demand for money away from transaction balances towards longer-term deposits. This is an illustration of the impact of cyclical variations in demand conditions which ought to be eliminated before one can regard a particular monetary aggregate as an indicator of policy influences.

On balance, conclusions with respect to any interpretation of German monetary aggregates as indicators of monetary thrust must necessarily remain less than firm. Their relationship to the preferred operating target of bank liquidity ratios has not been close over the shorter run, the main problems being caused by volatile capital flows. A further, though relatively minor, problem not touched upon in the above, is the tendency for loans from non-bank financial intermediaries — building and loan associations and insurance companies — to move procyclically. In periods of restraint, both these groups of institutions have found it possible to increase their lending; their ability to do so was enhanced by the tax incentives offered to depositors in building and loan associations, incentives which were sometimes improved in phases of restraint to encourage additional savings. Because of these important elements of flexibility in the German financial sector, it would be surprising if one could detect important effects of credit rationing on private expenditures. The sensitivity of capital flows to changes in relative monetary conditions implies, on the other hand, that the German monetary authorities dispose of powerful means of influencing the balance on non-monetary transactions (page 94). However, the predictability of the external position has been low because of large speculative flows.

Movements in industrial bond rates tended to coincide rather closely with those in the main indicator of short-term pressures in the money market, the interbank rate, as well as with changes in the discount rate.[1] The apparently quick response to changes in the main operating target of monetary policy, the bank liquidity ratio, reflects the importance of the banks in the bond market and the tendency for banks to react to a tightening of policy by initially reducing their acquisitions of bonds rather than their direct lending. This reaction pattern seems to have been particularly clear when reserve requirements were increased, while the influence of changes in rediscount quotas or the discount rate seems to have been somewhat weaker.[2] In 1960 and during part of 1966, banks actually reduced their holdings of bonds. The third restrictive phase was exceptional in that the interbank rate rose well above long-term rates and remained there for about one year; banks slowed down their purchases of bonds, but this was more than compensated by an upward shift in bond demands from the non-bank sector. These other buyers were apparently expecting the observed rise in rates to be only temporary; in fact, rates never came down significantly from their 1970 peak. Taking into account the accelerating price trends during this phase, it seems likely that the real cost of capital declined over most of 1969 and 1970.[3] In retrospect, the 1964–66 phase was the only one in which the increase in nominal bond yields ran clearly ahead of the acceleration in prices.

1. OECD Monetary Studies Series, *Monetary Policy in Germany*, pp. 67-68.
2. Multiplier results for the impact of various policy instruments on bank liquidity and some important interest rates are reported in work from the University of Mannheim, see H. König *et al.*, *An Econometric Model of the Financial Sector of the Federal Republic of Germany*, Parts I and II, Discussion Papers 38 and 39, 1973–74.
3. OECD Monetary Studies Series, *Monetary Policy in Germany*, p. 75; see also below, Part IV, page 106.

In the *United States*, the authorities have influenced the course of monetary aggregates mainly by open market operations. Observed growth rates of the two phases of monetary aggregates reflected quite clearly the two phases of monetary restraint in the 1960s (end-1965 to September 1966 and end-1968 to end-1969); this applied to both measures of the money supply, M1 and M2, and to total bank credit (Chart 20).[1] The pattern of response appears to have been very similar in these two phases. The picture is less clear in the two expansionary phases (March 1960 to end-1962 and end-1969 onwards). In the early phase the variables representing money market conditions, on which the authorities were relying as main short-term targets, all pointed strongly in the direction of ease during the initial months; from late 1960 the growth rate of all three aggregates remained stable. If one allows for the pick-up in aggregate demand following the through of the cycle in early 1961, these stable rates of expansion must have implied a gradual weakening of the expansionary thrust. In the later expansionary phase, when the monetary aggregates had become important targets in their own right, their rate of expansion had begun to accelerate even before the end of the preceding restrictive phase; the rate of growth of monetary aggregates became erratic in 1971.

Chart 20.   MONETARY AGGREGATES: UNITED STATES
Seasonally adjusted annual rate of change over previous quarter

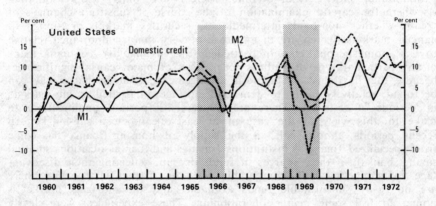

A large number of empirical studies have supplied evidence on the U.S. money supply process.[2] They suggest that non-borrowed reserves and short-term rates, notably the sensitive Federal funds rate, are the main determinants. The forecasting errors in predicting monthly observed changes in M1 from the supply side or with reduced form relations were sizeable − one half to one percentage point − over the months of 1970 and 1971, compared to actual growth rates ranging from -0.8 to +2.6 per cent per

1. OECD Monetary Studies Series, *Monetary Policy in the United States*, Part IV(d). Allowance for the influence of demand factors along the lines suggested by Hendershott's neutralized money stock also points to a clear weakening of the thrust from the aggregates in these phases; see *ibid.*, Chart. 18.
2. Some important contributions have been published in two volumes by the Federal Reserve Bank of Boston: *Controlling the Monetary Aggregates* I (1969) and II (1972).

month.[1] Month-to-month control of the aggregates is hardly feasible in the light of these results, as indeed the experiences in these years seemed to bear out. Furthermore, if the results of responses within the financial sector were taken literally, the estimated relations imply that very substantial gyrations in short-term rates would have to be tolerated to achieve steady monthly growth rates of M1. For example, one of these short-term models[2] suggests that in 1971 it would have needed a lowering of the Federal funds rate by nearly 400 basis points to boost the observed money stock by $1 billion (or approximately 0.5 per cent) in the course of one month. If the $1 billion changes were required only after three months, the Federal funds rate would have had to drop only by 70 basis points. The required interest rate adjustment would be further halved by aiming at achieving an M1 target over a time horizon of 6-7 months by which time the money market should adjust fully (still abstracting from any impact of the rate change through feedback from the real economy to the financial sector). Such calculations, if roughly correct, underline the importance of allowing for the lapse of at least some months in designing an aggregate target.

The United States financial sector is highly competitive and flexible. Compared with other countries surveyed, it is on the whole a close approximation to the textbook version of an integrated or "perfect" financial market in which sub-markets are cleared by adjustments in interest rates within rather short periods of time. There is accordingly less reason than elsewhere for careful examination of the course of substitute channels of credit, whether non-bank intermediaries, securities markets or foreign financial markets (which are in any case of very minor importance relative to U.S. domestic markets). In particular, the "availability" of bank loans of any particular type of credit is not in itself of major causal significance, because the flexibility of financial arrangements assumes that a way can be found, relatively easily, to stem fund shortages in particular sub-markets in periods of restraint. There are, however, important qualifications to make to this view in the case of at least one financial sub-market. In recent periods almost half of the supply of housing finance has come from specialized financial institutions (savings and loan associations, mutual savings banks); if their sources of funds dry up, reflecting their disadvantage in competing with comparable rates on market instruments, there are no easily substitutable funds available, and the mortgage market is bound to feel some degree of rationing. These experiences were clearly revealed in the two phases of restraint in 1966 and 1969. More generally the mechanism may be illustrated by means of simulation experiments with a comprehensive model of the financial sector which allows for selected availability effects.[3] During the first few quarters after an increase in the Treasury bill rate — chosen to represent an operating target — the availability of housing finance declines; after about four quarters the effects begin to fade, as the specialized institutions become able to adjust upwards the rates they offer to depositors. As explained above (page 44), a major

1. Pierce and Thomson, *Controlling the Monetary Aggregates* II, p. 126.
2. Work by R. Davis, quoted by Pierce and Thomson. See also R. Davis, "Short-run Targets for Open Market Operations" in *Open Market Policies and Operating Procedures*, Staff Studies, Federal Reserve Board 1971, and "Implementing Open Market Policy with Monetary Aggregate Objectives", *Monthly Review of the Federal Reserve Bank of New York*, July 1973.
3. OECD Monetary Studies Series, *Monetary Policy in the United States*, Chart 13.

reason for using some direct administrative control over interest rates in the United States has been to prevent availability effects in the housing market from reaching disproportionate levels.

Chart 21. THE STRUCTURE OF INTEREST RATES:
UNITED STATES

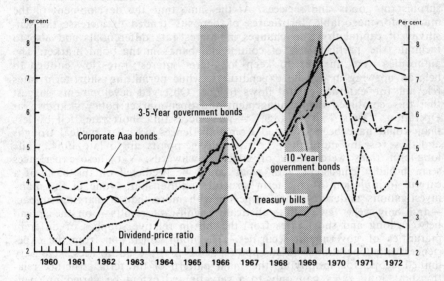

A review of the term structure of interest rates (Chart 21) may usefully take its point of departure in the Treasury bill rates, one of the main elements of money market conditions and as such an important policy target. If one assumes that the bill rate has, to a close approximation, been controlled through open market operations, it is possible to review by means of policy simulations the consequences for other interest rates of, say, a more restrictive monetary policy. The following remarks are based on simulations with the quarterly model of U.S. economy developed jointly by the Federal Reserve System, the Massachussetts Institute of Technology and the University of Pennsylvania (the "FMP" model). The commercial paper rate, which is an important indicator of short-term marginal borrowing costs for corporations, adjusts very quickly and more than fully to the increase in the bill rate. From the commercial paper rate, the effect spreads very gradually to longer-term markets; the adjustment is a prolonged one, lasting 4-5 years in the FMP model and nearly as long in several other empirical studies. At the end of the first year, the corporate bond yield has risen only by one third of the original (and sustained) increase in the bill rate and other interest rates – and the dividend/price ratio by even less. In the long run, i.e. over 4-5 years, the corporate bond rate adjusts by nearly the same number of percentage points as the bill rate, but the time lag is clearly so long as to make this conclusion of limited interest from a practical policy viewpoint. This implies that, in order to achieve significant shifts in long rates within a relevant policy horizon, say one year at the most, short rates have to change quite drastically. Since this is undesirable from the viewpoint of ensuring financial stability, the results yield some negative implications for policy.[1]

During 1961–64 the U.S. authorities designed their open market operations and debt management policies so as to modify gently the term structure relationship. During this period the economy was operating below full capacity; but there was also an external deficit, as net outflows of capital coupled with official transfers significantly exceeded the shrinking surplus on goods and services. At the same time the development of the market for negotiable certificates of deposits tended to increase the sensitivity of capital flows to changes in interest rate differentials and also to facilitate the participation of commercial banks in the bond market. The authorities were anxious to keep long-term interest rates low enough to help an upswing in private expenditures, while permitting short-term rates relevant for external capital flows to rise. Observed developments suggest that this combined debt-management and open-market policy – known as Operation "Twist" or "Nudge" – was successful. Short rates fell by less than would have been expected from experiences in earlier cyclical troughs and they rose by more than 1.50 percentage points up to late 1964, while long-term rates were stable or edged downwards. Yet these experiences seem broadly consistent with what could be predicted on the basis of a careful formulation of the term structure relationship. None of the many investigations undertaken has come up with more than a marginal impact – and only very few with statistically significant results – on the spread between long and short rates from the shift in relative supplies of different maturities of government securities.[2] The main conclusion from the experiences with Operations Twist appears to be that the authorities have very limited scope for modifying the main pattern of the term structure relationship; long rates can only to a very limited extent be varied independently of short rates. The conclusion is tentative, since it is conceivable that larger shifts in the maturity composition of the public debt than the relatively modest steps taken in 1961 might have left an impact.

As explained above (pages 62-63), the design of monetary policy in the *United Kingdom* has been modified in recent years. Prior to 1968–69 bank credit expansion was a major policy target. As shown in Chart 22,[3] the monetary restraint in 1960–61 and its subsequent removal were both clearly reflected in the growth rate of the narrow money supply (M1). During 1965–66, bank credit started to decelerate around mid-1965; the deceleration of M1 which had started earlier in the year seems to have been prompted by the deterioration of the balance of payments. Both aggregates picked up rather strongly in 1967 after the end of restraint early that year. When policy was tightened once more at the time of the November 1967 devaluation, the slowdown in M1 at the initial stage of restraint was again largely due to external deficits; despite the use of credit ceilings, it was only in the second half of 1968 that bank credit

1. Empirical work in relation to the FMP model suggests one further reason why sharp changes in short rates may be undesirable. Instability of short rates adds to the risk premium required by holders of longer-term assets; it therefore widens, *ceteris paribus*, the spread between long and short rates. This would be undesirable in a situation where the authorities were aiming to lower long rates by pushing bill rates down.
2. OECD Monetary Studies Series, *Monetary Policy in the United States*, Appendix IV.
3. Because of statistical problems, the developments of domestic credit and the broadest money stock (M3) are shown only from mid-1963.

started to decelerate (see also page 42). During this period of restraint, the interest of the authorities shifted towards broader aggregates; the concept used was at first domestic credit expansion (DCE), subsequently both DCE and a broad measure of the money stock (M3).[1] Since the introduction of the reform in *Competition and Credit Control*, the authorities have been commenting on developments in all three series, displaying an eclecticism as pronounced as that of the Federal Reserve System during the period in which an aggregate-based strategy prevailed (page 54).

Chart 22.   MONETARY AGGREGATES: UNITED KINGDOM
Seasonally adjusted annual rate of change over previous quarter

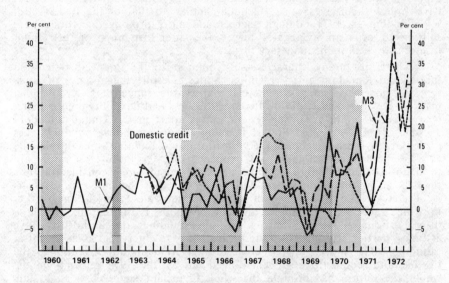

There was some basis for arguing that M3 was a rough indicator of monetary thrust prior to 1971; the influence of policy factors on M3 was clearly greater than on M1 which tended to be more susceptible to shifts in the demand for transactions balances. One inevitable — and deliberate — consequence of *Competition and Credit Control* was to allow bank lending to make a major upward adjustment during a process of reintermediation, as banks recaptured a larger share of financial flows, previously limited by ceilings and other restrictive arrangements. Since there is no analytically satisfactory way of assessing the duration of this adjustment and its size in any particular period, the usefulness of M3 as an indicator of monetary thrust was seriously impaired. A further source of difficulties in the interpretation of M3 is the inclusion of sterling certificates of deposits, the attractive yield on which prompted the so-called "merry-go-round" in 1972-73 — a process through which some bank customers found it to their advantage to make use of their overdraft facilities for investment in CDs.

1. "Key issues in monetary and credit policy", a speech by the Governor, *Bank of England Quarterly Bulletin*, June 1971.

The December 1973 " supplementary scheme " based on the increase in interest-earning liabilities in excess of that recommended by the Bank of England (page 64) helped to stem the "merry-go-round". At the same time the clearing banks announced that they were taking steps to discontinue the arbitrage by linking the rate charged of some customers to money market rates. The unwinding of this special factor tended to slow down the growth rate of M3; the period over which this aggregate supplies unreliable information about monetary thrust is accordingly extended. Therefore, any firm interpretation of the causal significance of the generally high and volatile growth rates of M3 and domestic credit since 1971 would be hazardous. There is some evidence of upward shifts in both supply and demand,[1] although controversies remain on the role of the supply shift in recent volatile developments of M3. The U.K. authorities have found themselves in a dilemma similar to that of the Federal Reserve System in 1971, though sharper and more prolonged: as they were shifting towards an aggregates target, the latter lost much of their significance as indicators of monetary thrust.

There are many characteristics common to the financial systems in the United Kingdom and the United States. Despite the absence of some types of assets, notably commercial paper, the range of U.K. financial markets is wider, and features of competitiveness and flexibility predominate. One segment of the financial system stands apart in the United Kingdom as well as in the United States. Lending for private house building takes place largely through specialized institutions – building societies in the case of the United Kingdom. As explained on page 46, interest rates paid to depositors in building societies have tended to move considerably less than those on competing assets with the result that the inflow of deposits is severely reduced at times of rising market rates. This is one market in which access to substitute sources of funds is limited; to prevent a disproportionately strong impact on housebuilding, the authorities have at times, particularly in 1973, found it necessary to intervene so as to offset rationing.[2] The mortgage market accordingly remains an exception to the flexible and competitive system aimed at by the 1971 reform. On the whole, the reform has brought the whole financial system closer to a state such as that exemplified in the United States where observed flows of credit have taken on more of a descriptive rather than a causal significance. But exceptions have remained also outside the mortgage market – qualitative guidance in the form of " priority " lending having encouraged this – and the recent moves towards more direct forms of control have checked the trend towards the high degree of flexibility originally aimed at before the movement had been completed.

The term structure of interest rates in the market for U.K. Government securities suggests, as is the case for the U.S. market, that expec-

---

1. This is the interpretation of a recent study – M.J. Artis and M.K. Lewis, "The Demand for Money: Stable or Unstable?", *The Banker*, March 1974 – in some conflict with the emphasis on a demand explanation implicit in " Does the Money Supply Really Matter?", a speech by the Deputy Governor, *Bank of England Quarterly Bulletin*, June 1973; and with the result of an econometric study by the Bank of England, G. Haache, " The Demand for Money in the United Kingdom: Experience since 1971 ", *Bank of England Quarterly Bulletin*, September 1974.

2. In September 1973 the government placed a limit of 9.50 per cent on the rate which banks can pay on deposit accounts of less than £10,000 (page 46). In view of the net outflow of funds from the building societies in the early months of 1974, the government started in May to extend a loan to the societies in order to maintain their interest rates at relatively low levels.

tational factors play the most important role. Empirical studies, many of them by economists at the Bank of England[1] have accounted fairly well for most of the observed fluctuations in the yield gap, i.e. the spread between long and short rates; no major modification of the pattern of rates has been detected following the 1971 reform. Chart 23 shows the yield on three important Government debt instruments: Treasury bills, 5-year and 20-year. The relationship between the latter two has been rather close, indicating that the yield curve has normally been rather flat in this range. A gap opened up in 1970–71, but it seems to have been attributable to a few observable factors, notably recent price changes and capital gains taxation. There has been only a very short lead of the 5-year over the 20-year rate, somewhat contrary to the findings in the United States. The bill rate has fluctuated substantially more than the longer-term rates, but, here too, the lead seems to be shorter than the long drawn-out response found in the United States (page 79). The link from the bill rate to longer-term rates is not yet well established empirically. But since the authorities intervene quite actively in the market for shorter-dated government stocks, this does not imply the lack of influence on rates outside the shortest end of the market.[2] The greater freedom of action claimed by the Bank in its securities dealings under Competition and Credit Control underlines that the post-1971 design of policy may be expected to allow larger countercyclical variations in longer-term rates.

While the conclusions on the overall contribution of monetary policy to short-run management of the economy will be left for Part V, a summing up of some of the findings with respect to the impact on domestic financial variables may be useful before proceeding, in Part IV, to an examination of the impact on expenditure flows and other ultimate objectives of policy. The diversity of the six economies surveyed makes such a summary difficult; the differences between the way changes in monetary policy instruments influence the course of monetary aggregates and longer-term interest rates – the two main candidates as indicators of monetary thrust surveyed in the present section – are quite striking. While there are only very few examples of the authorities " losing control " over one or the other of these indicators in the sense of making them move procyclically, the time lags involved tend to be long and to vary substantially. Generally, the degree of control over the monetary aggregates has been prompter and more accurate in countries relying on credit ceilings than in those operating more indirectly through changes in reserve money and short-term interest rates. Yet the experiences of the United States suggest that the impact on the aggregates can be made predictable to a fairly high degree if one is content with aiming for a 3 to 6 month horizon and that

1. Notably J.P. Burman and W.R. White, " Yield curves for gilt-edged stocks ", *Bank of England Quarterly Bulletin*, December 1972; J.P. Burman, " Yield curves for gilt-edged stocks: further investigation ", *ibid.*, September 1973; M. Hamburger, " Expectations, long-term interest rates and monetary policy in the United Kingdom ", *ibid.*, September 1971; and C.A.E. Goodhart and D. Gowland, " The relationship between the yield on long and short-dated gilt-edged stocks ", *unpublished* 1973.
2. As noted above (page 28) the Treasury bill market has been shrinking in relative importance in recent years and the bill rate has become less representative of short-term financial pressures. This process has been furthered by the 1971 reform, which has tended to lower the bill rate relative to other short rates in periods of tightening. It may be more fruitful, therefore, to formulate term-structure relationships that depart from short rates outside the Treasury bill market; the local authority rate is an important candidate.

Chart 23. THE STRUCTURE OF INTEREST RATES : UNITED KINGDOM

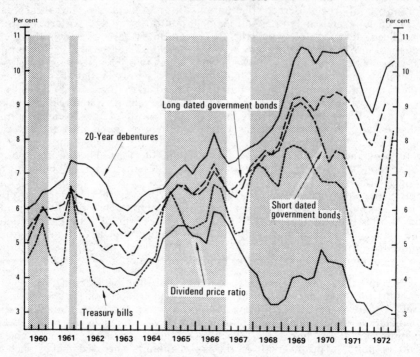

such a policy need not impose unacceptable strain on short-term financial markets. As regards the impact on longer-term interest rates the record is also mixed, ranging from the direct impact through open market operations at the long end (Italy) or consultations with the authorities (Japan, France) to the very indirect one in the United States, where the observed course of long-term rates is well explained by movements in short-term rates, but with time lags so long as to rule out any large policy-engineered shift in nominal bond yields over any shorter period. These time lags may be shortened if, as in Germany, there is a significant group of financial institutions active in the markets for both securities and money.

The significance of these conclusions can be assessed only in the light of the further links from the two groups of indicators to the components of demand. It is premature to conclude, say, that monetary policy in country A is less efficient than in country B because long-term interest rates or the rates of growth of bank credit are less directly influenceable through policy: the sensitivity of final demand to any given change in one of these indicators may be sufficiently greater in country A to offset this apparent disadvantage. It is the purpose of Part IV to assess selected parts of the available evidence on this real impact. Finally, it may be worthwhile recalling that even if it could be demonstrated that the greater degree of control over an indicator of monetary thrust combined with the evidence of the real impact made monetary policy a more effective stabilization tool in country B than in country A, this would still fall short of an implicit recommendation to adjust the design of policy in A to that of

B. Efficiency in a stabilization tool is one important property to be desired. But there are others, notably the promotion of competition and efficiency in the financial sector, which may be in conflict with it. This conflict was exemplified in the United Kingdom in the debate on the Competition and Credit Control reform. That the degree of control over the monetary aggregates was at least temporarily weakened by the reform can hardly be denied; but without an assessment of the benefits in efficiency terms of removing the earlier ceiling system, no verdict on the reform can be made. The 'task of the present study is only the partial one to assess the stabilization features of monetary policy.

B.   IMPACT ON EXTERNAL CAPITAL FLOWS

As already indicated briefly in the preceding section, the degree of control over external capital flows is one important determinant of the accuracy with which the authorities can hope to influence the course of the money supply and total credit flows. Indeed, the sensitivity of capital flows to changes in differentials between domestic and foreign interest rates is an important constraint on the extent to which interest rate targets can be geared to domestic policy objectives. But at the same time, capital flows are in themselves an important policy target, since they determine together with the current account of the balance of payments the change in a country's international reserves. There is a trade-off between the efficiency of policy instruments in relation to these two roles of capital flows; the greater the efficiency of, say, discount rate changes, in keeping international reserves on a desired course, the more limited their domestic efficiency.

These considerations suggest that it would be useful to review, in more detail than in the preceding section, the experiences of the six countries with respect to the sensitivity and volatility of external capital flows. The following survey will be introduced by the experiences of the two countries, Japan and France, which appear to have been faced with the least volatile capital flows, mainly because of extensive regulations. *A priori*, one would expect the conditions for controlling the monetary aggregates to be more favourable; the experiences of the two countries with credit ceilings or comparable instruments suggest that this is indeed the case. The United States is a special case; though interest-sensitive capital flows have clearly been regarded as a significant constraint on monetary policy in some phases, the institutional characteristics of the international monetary system – the dominant role of the dollar in international reserve creation – and the huge size of U.S. financial markets relative to external transactions combined to bring about a high degree of insulation of these markets, making it feasible to aim at domestically designed targets for interest rates or monetary aggregates. The three remaining countries, Italy, the United Kingdom and Germany, have been the least able to disregard external constraints in active phases of policy.

Turning to the experiences of individual countries, *Japan* again represents an extreme case; a variety of programmes have tended to keep total net flows within narrow bounds despite substantial shifts in relative monetary conditions in Japan and elsewhere[1] (Chart 24). The outflow of

1.   OECD Monetary Studies Series, *Monetary Policy in Japan*, pp. 38-43.

Chart 24.   INTEREST RATES AND CAPITAL FLOWS:
JAPAN

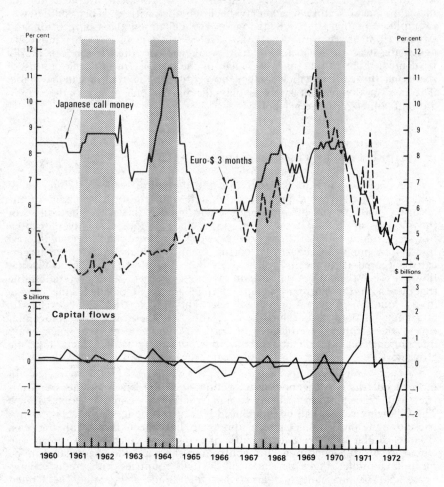

long-term domestic capital was generally consistent with relative monetary
conditions in Japan and other markets, but it is difficult to separate the
effect of changing monetary conditions from the impact of exchange controls. More recently, the flow of long-term domestic capital was influenced
by the authorities' special transactions. Exchange controls have also modified the influence of relative monetary conditions on the flow of non-
monetary short-term capital – a large inflow of such capital in the period
1971–72 was motivated by speculative activity rather than interest arbitrage.
In restrictive periods, the inflow of banking funds was also contained within
narrow ranges; the authorities limited the banks' conversion of externally
raised funds for domestic use. In easy periods, the authorities relaxed the
controls and let market forces (the difference between monetary conditions
at home and abroad, the volume of exports and imports, etc.) work more
freely in determining the flow of capital. A large inflow of banking funds
after the announcement of the United States' new balance of payments

programme in 1971 was unrelated to the stance of monetary policy which was then expansionary.

There is some econometric evidence on the influence of interest rates on Japanese short-term capital flows, but the interest sensitivity has been generally very small because of exchange control measures. A study covering the 1960s[1] concluded that a one-point rise in the differential between the Japanese money market rates and Euro-dollar rates would bring a capital inflow of about $100 million. Half of that sum would come in the first quarter following the change, and the other half in the succeeding three months; sixty per cent of the total inflow would be concentrated in the movement of banking funds. Another study,[2] focusing only on Japanese borrowing from the United States banking system, also found some influence from relative interest rates, although changes in capital controls accounted for about 70 per cent of the variation in such borrowing.

In *France*, flows of long-term and non-monetary short-term capital as well as banking funds, which had remained within narrow ranges up to 1966, were influenced more importantly by market forces in the following years when capital control measures were discontinued[3] (Chart 25). While a large outflow of long-term and non-monetary short-term capital in 1968 was essentially motivated by exchange rate expectations, net inflows between mid-1969 and mid-1970 seem to have reflected relatively tighter domestic monetary conditions, although the initial reflows may have been partly the result of the unwinding of speculative activity. During this period the corporate sector made extensive use of long-term borrowing abroad which was permitted by the authorities to reconstitute foreign exchange reserves. For the same reasons, corporations increased borrowing from their foreign suppliers and foreign banks until exchange controls introduced in July 1970 prevented residents from borrowing abroad for less than one year. In subsequent years, the visual correlation with relative monetary conditions was again destroyed by strong speculative activity.

The movement of banking funds in the 1968–69 period when the French banks were free from exchange control regulations was also the result of speculation rather than arbitrage activity. The inflow of banking funds in 1970 was, on the other hand, generally consistent with relative monetary conditions in France and other markets. But it is difficult to distinguish the impact of the change in relative monetary conditions from the effect of the regulation on the banks' foreign exchange position introduced at the end of 1969. Banking funds moved violently again as a result of speculative activity in the subsequent years until a free market for the financial franc was introduced in August 1971. The rates which are generally considered to be most important for arbitrage operations are the French short-term money market rates and Euro-currency deposit rates. However, partly because of frequent changes in exchange control measures, no econometric study testing the interest-sensitivity of capital flows has produced convincing results.

An important fact to be taken into account in analysing the interest-sensitivity of the capital account for *Italy* is the absence of an active domestic money market. Surplus short-term funds in commercial banks or

1. A. Amano, *International Capital Movements: Theory and Estimation*, Kobe University (unpublished).
2. R.C. Bryant and P.H. Hendershott, "Financial Capital Flows in the Balance of Payments of the United States: An Exploratory Empirical Study", *Princeton Studies in International Finance*, No. 25, International Finance Section, Princeton University, 1970.
3. OECD Monetary Studies Series, *Monetary Policy in France*, Part IV.B.

Chart 25. INTEREST RATES AND CAPITAL FLOWS:
FRANCE

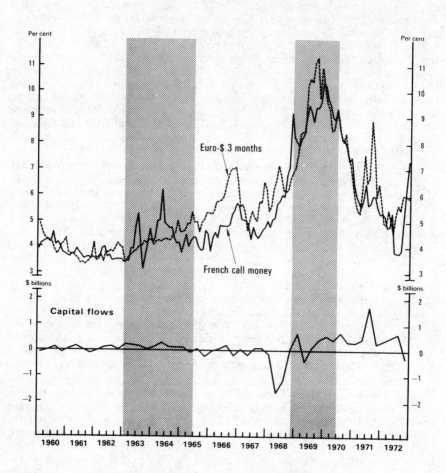

special credit institutions are either invested in deposits with one of the
larger banks or a central credit institution, in Treasury bills or, provided
that the possibility has not been excluded by the Bank of Italy's regulation
on the banks' external position, in foreign money markets. Interest rates
in the inter-bank deposit market were subject to a legal maximum between
1962 and 1969; the Treasury bill rate was completely stabilized until May
1969, and the discount rate was not changed. The authorities assumed a
more flexible attitude to short-term interest rate policy from 1969, but
conjunctural difficulties have so far prevented any important development
of the money market. This means that the flow of interest-sensitive
banking funds has until recently been influenced primarily by foreign rates,
notably the Euro-dollar rate (Chart 26) within the limit set by official
control on the banks' foreign position. On the other hand, Italian markets
for long-term finance are well developed and both banks and non-bank
sectors are active participants in those markets. Domestic long-term rates

Chart 26. INTEREST RATES AND CAPITAL FLOWS:
ITALY

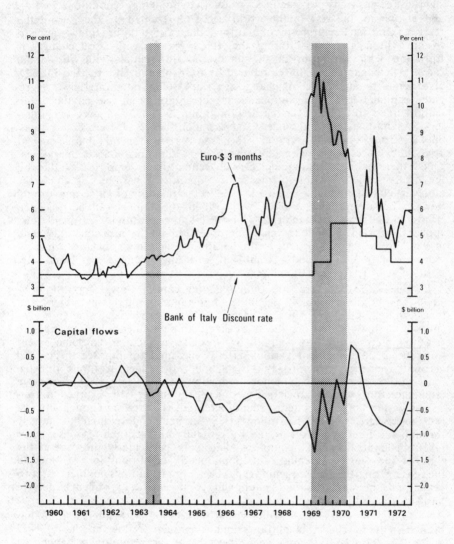

have generally moved more flexibly than short rates, although a policy of pegging long-term bond rates was followed in the period mid-1966 to mid-1969 and from mid-1973 onwards. The scope for compensating changes in the availability of domestic credit by fluctuations in long-term capital inflows remained circumscribed; still there was some tendency for net long-term inflows to rise in 1969–1970. The same was the case for short-term flows prior to the end of 1966 when restrictions were temporarily lifted; they were largely reintroduced in 1968 to stem outflows. In the course of 1969 capital flows gradually changed direction, and up to 1972 the main aim was to limit inflows.

89

Though holdings of foreign exchange by non-bank residents have been subject to controls, several empirical studies reinforce the impression of a significant sensitivity to changes in relative monetary conditions in Italy and elsewhere, the rest of the world being represented by the Euro-dollar market. One particular form of outflow, the export of lira notes, appears to have been associated during the 1960s mainly with fiscal changes in Italy and with variations in the uncovered differentials with Euro-dollar rates.[1] The econometric study prepared by Branson and Hill for the OECD[2] also points to an impact of changes in Euro-dollar rates on Italy's aggregated capital account; a sustained one percentage point rise on the differential tended to generate an outflow of about $400 million over two quarters. A third study[3] finds a less significant influence of Euro-dollar rates, but a strong impact from the other sources of monetary base: current account balance, net government transactions and open market operations. Thus, there is not full agreement between available empirical studies on the relative role of interest rates and "quantity" variables, such as the monetary base or bank credit, in the determination of offsetting capital flows. The degree of accuracy with which the impact can be predicted is also less than satisfactory. Nevertheless the sensitivity of such flows appears sufficiently high to make manipulation of the monetary base and interest rates an important means of adjusting Italy's balance on non-monetary transactions and — combined with the regulation of banks' net position — official international reserves.

The salient feature of *United States* capital flows since the mid-1960s has been the rapidly declining importance of direct investment and long-term capital movements in general and the progressive dominance of short-term flows which are the more likely to be influenced by changes in relative interest rates as well as by speculative factors. To some extent this reflects the impact of various selective measures to improve the capital account over the years 1963-1973 (page 50); these measures were directed more at long-term than at short-term flows. Until late 1969 short-term (and therefore total financial) flows generally moved in a direction consistent with changes in interest rate differentials (Chart 27).[4] Though interest rates elsewhere tended to follow U.S. monetary developments, largely through the intermediation of the Euro-dollar market, such responses were far from immediate and complete. This was particularly the case at the time of the sharp tightening of U.S. monetary conditions in 1968-69 and the easing in the subsequent year. The capital inflows in the first two years and the outflows in the following year can be explained largely in terms of relative interest rates.

In recent years, the strong visual correlation with interest rates has been destroyed. The large outflows and subsequent reflows in the 1971-72 and 1972-73 periods seem to have been more the result of exchange-rate expectations than of relative monetary conditions. It is tempting to suppose that the total capital inflow of $12.7 billion to the United States in

1. F. Vicarelli, "L'Esportazione di Bancnote nell'Esperianza Italiana dell'Ultimo Decennio", *Studi Economici 1970.* The use of forward cover is negligible in Italy.
2. W.H. Branson and R.D. Hill, Jr., "Capital Movements in the OECD Area", *OECD Economic Outlook, Occasional Studies*, December 1971.
3. P. Kouri and M. Porter, "International Capital Flows and Portfolio Equilibrium", *unpublished* paper presented at the annual meeting of Project LINK, Vienna, September 1972.
4. OECD Monetary Studies Series, *Monetary Policy in the United States*, Part III (e).

Chart 27. INTEREST RATES AND CAPITAL FLOWS:
UNITED STATES

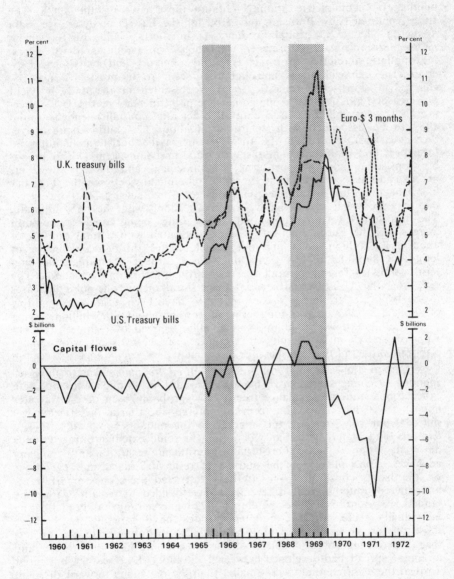

1973 was a consequence of the sharp rise in interest rates in that country. However, when account is taken of the even greater increases in foreign rates, it appears more likely that the purely monetary influence was slightly negative for the United States in the year 1973 as a whole. The major exception to that pattern was the inflow of foreign funds to the United States in the second quarter of 1973, when a fall in U.K. interest rates coincided with the still rising U.S. rates.

The interest-sensitivity of financial capital movements in general and short-term capital flows in particular has been shown to be high in a number of econometric studies, notably those covering the 1960s. The study conducted by Branson and Hill for the OECD analyses five main items on the U.S. capital account: *i*) short-term claims on foreigners, *ii*) long-term claims on foreigners, *iii*) short-term liabilities to foreigners, *iv*) long-term liabilities to foreigners, and *v*) errors and omissions. U.S. short-term financial assets and liabilities seem to be most influenced by changes in short-term domestic rates (represented in the study by yields on Treasory bills). Thus a one-percentage point increase in the U.S. three-month Treasury bill rate (assuming all other rates constant) tended around 1969 to be associated with an inflow of about $2.5 billion (spread over three quarters), mostly in the form of increased short-term liabilities to foreigners and of increases in the errors and omissions item (which probably consists mainly of short-term non-monetary capital). It is, however, necessary to take into account the close relationship between the Treasury bill rate and Euro-dollar rates; empirical evidence suggests that the three-month Euro-dollar rate is likely to increase along with the U.S. bill rate. The Branson-Hill study finds that, other things being equal, a one-point increase in the Euro-dollar rate will be associated with a total outflow of about $1.1 billion, of which one fourth comes through a reduction of long-term liabilities to foreigners, one fourth through an increase in long-term claims on foreigners, and the rest through errors and omissions. The effect on the U.S. capital account from simultaneous one-point increases in the two rates around 1969 is estimated to have been a short-term inflow of about $2 billion and a long-term outflow of about $0.5 billion, giving a net total inflow of about $1.50 billion spread over three quarters.[1] Approximately similar results are found in a recent study with a more elaborate model of the U.S. balance of payments.[2]

Capital flows in and out of the *United Kingdom* seem to have responded to changes in relative monetary conditions, though exchange rate expectations and trade balance trends have probably been of even greater importance (Chart 28). The form of foreign short-term investments has shifted from the Treasury bill market to the markets for local authority deposits and, later, inter-bank deposits; to some extent arbitraged funds have also moved into short-term Government securities and company advances. The controls on the outflow of residents' funds and regulations on the banks' position (page 50) have restricted the scope for arbitrage, and covered interest rate differentials have tended to remain against the United Kingdom. Since the middle of 1972 while sterling has been floating individually, U.K. short-term interest rates have generally been above those on foreign assets; in late 1973 the local authorities rate was no less than 5 percentage points higher than the three-month Euro-dollar rate, and a similar spread had developed between U.S. and U.K. Treasury bill rates. Though these differentials were smaller than the prevailing forward discount on sterling, a sizeable inflow of capital was nevertheless achieved.

While the Branson and Hill study for the OECD failed to uncover a positive relationship between the U.K. local authority rate and net

1. According to the study, no other national long rates have proved significant in the U.S. equations, although the U.S. bond rate is used as a variable in explaining the German and Canadian capital accounts.
2. S.Y. Kwack, "The Impact of the Smithsonian Exchange Rate Agreement on the U.S. Balance of Payments: An Econometric Analysis", *unpublished*, March 1974, Table 5.

Chart 28. INTEREST RATES AND CAPITAL FLOWS:
UNITED KINGDOM

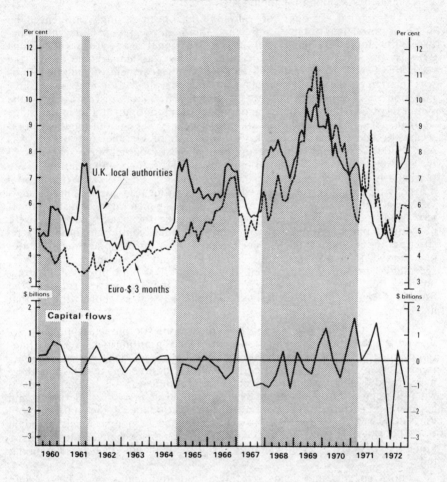

capital inflows to the United Kingdom, other work focusing on short-term flows has pointed to a sensitivity in quarterly flows to changes in the differential. One study, focusing on the mid-1960s, found that a one-point rise in the local authorities rate over the Euro-dollar rate would generate an inflow of about $300 million.[1] Another study found the demand for money by U.K. residents to have been highly sensitive to the **Euro-dollar rate** (as well as to domestic income and long-term rates).[2] These results underline the openness of the U.K. financial sector despite the relatively tight control of residents' foreign transactions. However,

1. Z. Hodjera, "Short-Term Capital Movements of the United Kingdom 1963–1967", *Journal of Political Economy*, July-August 1971.
2. M. Hamburger, "The Demand for Money in an Open Economy: Germany and the United Kingdom", *unpublished*, April 1974.

there are still some uncertainties about the role of foreign interests in U.K. residents' demand for money.[1]

The capital account of *Germany* has been strongly influenced by domestic monetary policy, reflecting the high degree of integration between the domestic credit system and international financial markets (Chart 29). The problem of stemming capital inflows was manageable during the restrictive period from mid-1964 to 1966. The movement of banking funds was contained by various measures, and the inflow of interest-sensitive non-monetary capital, which was essentially free, was discouraged by the simultaneous tightening of monetary conditions abroad at the initial stage of that period; a large inflow of non-monetary capital during this period seems to have been related to the upsurge of German imports. It was only in the latter part of the period that interest-induced borrowing abroad by German companies occurred on a substantial scale. Capital inflows were particularly large during the restrictive period of 1969–1971. While capital movements during this period were largely influenced by speculative activity, the inflows in 1970 and early 1971,[2] which were basically short-term and took place both through and outside the banking system, were no doubt partly connected with the fact that continuous monetary restriction in Germany and the decline of international money market rates had turned interest differentials largely in favour of Germany. Moreover, speculative pressure strengthened the forward DM and provided a strong incentive to covered interest arbitrage; it also lowered interest rates on the Euro-DM market and encouraged German companies' borrowing in that market.

Partly to limit the extent to which domestic monetary policies are upset by international capital flows, the German authorities have instituted programmes of control on the flow of non-bank capital as well as banking funds during times when restriction has been desired (page 49). But these measures did not prevent a substantial capital inflow ($4.3 billion) in 1973, when there was both a large interest differential in favour of Germany and a general expectation of a continued rise in the value of the mark. Indeed the inflow might have been even larger had it not been cushioned in 1973 by the relatively free movement of German exchange rates vis-à-vis non-" snake " currencies in response to shifting demands for mark-denominated assets.

Both covered and uncovered interest rate differentials have been found useful in explaining German capital flows (see above). One study for the IMF found a large impact from the covered differential between German money market rates and Euro-dollar rates: over a three-month period, a one-point rise in that differential was estimated to generate an inflow of some $0.75 billion of short-term capital within a month. Taking into account the lagged adjustments in the following months, the total effect appears to be 3-4 times as large.[3] Branson and Hill found a relationship of roughly the same magnitude for the uncovered rate differentials between

1. A recent study by the Bank of England reports that an attempt to incorporate the Euro-dollar rate as an explanatory variable in the U.K. demand for money function was less successful. See G. Haache, *op. cit.*

2. In the restrictive period from early 1970 to December of that year, the external effects were nearly 1.5 times as large as the January 1970 volume of bank liquidity; by May 1971, the effects were more than 2.5 times as large (see OECD Monetary Studies Series, *Monetary Policy in Germany*, p. 64).

3. M. Porter, "Capital Flows as an Offset to Monetary Policy: The German Experience", *IMF Staff Papers*, July 1972.

Chart 29.   INTEREST RATES AND CAPITAL FLOWS:
GERMANY

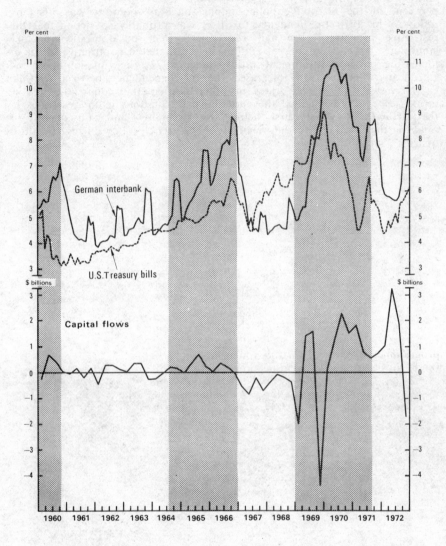

the U.S. Government securities market and German inter-bank and bond
markets, but — surprisingly — no independent influence from the Euro-
dollar rate. Recent work by Hamburger on the demand for money function
in Germany finds the covered Euro-dollar deposit rate to be an important
determinant of money demand, almost on a par with German short-term
rates; this confirms the impression of a very high degree of interest sensitivity in capital flows.[1] A similar conclusion has been reached in other

1. M. Hamburger, *op. cit.* One debatable feature in this as in several other studies is
that the short-term German rate used — the inter-bank rate — is, strictly speaking, relevant only for the analysis of bank portfolios.

empirical studies by economists in Germany and at the IMF. Thus, a study done at the IMF suggests that on the average as much as 80-85 per cent of the restrictive policy impact on bank liquidity was offset by inflows.[1] In 1970 the tendency to offset was probably so strong that the restrictive measures taken had a perverse effect on domestic monetary conditions by encouraging an inflow larger than the contractive effect of increasing reserve requirement ratios. Since 1972, the functioning of the European " Snake " has increased the interdependence between German capital flows and interest rates in other participating countries. Notable influences in 1973 included the very sharp fluctuations in interest rates in the Netherlands which first helped to strengthen and subsequently to weaken the mark and the relatively low French rates during the third quarter.

---

1. See the references given in OECD Monetary Studies Series, *Monetary Policy in Germany*, p. 65.

IV

IMPACT OF MONETARY POLICY
ON AGGREGATE DEMAND AND ITS COMPONENTS

A.   IMPACT ON MAIN COMPONENTS OF PRIVATE EXPENDITURE

This section examines the role of monetary policy in the determination of private expenditures in the six major countries, focusing on four main components: *i*) fixed non-residential investment; *ii*) inventory investment; *iii*) residential investment; and *iv*) consumption.[1] The visual observation of the cyclical pattern of these expenditures in various phases of monetary policy will be followed by an assessment, insofar as possible, of the sensitivity of each component of private expenditures to monetary influences. A review will also be made of the process through which monetary policy changes are transmitted to private spending.

The measurement of the effects of monetary policy changes on individual demand components — the total impact and its pattern over time — is a crucial policy issue, since the authorities are concerned not only with the cyclical adjustment of aggregate demand, but also with its composition. There are three main considerations. First, precise knowledge of various sectoral effects of monetary policy will help the authorities in designing monetary policy and choosing a combination of fiscal and other measures to attain the short-run objective of stabilizing aggregate demand and simultaneously to achieve the longer-run policy aim of insulating particular demand components from the undesirable effects of monetary policy. Secondly, if the time lags for policy actions to affect expenditure are long, the use of monetary policy for anti-cyclical purposes will necessitate the authorities' capacity to forecast autonomous cyclical movements over a long time horizon and to take counter-cyclical monetary actions well before the actual observation of cyclical turning points. Since such forecasting is difficult, monetary policy actions involving long time lags may be poorly suited for short-run stabilization. Thirdly, an important problem for policy relates to the identification of the transmission process of monetary policy. The specification of particular financial variables which are directly linked with the real sector will enable the authorities to choose appropriate financial targets which minimize the degree of variability or instability of the ultimate effects of monetary policy changes.

---

1. In this section, these expenditures are generally examined in real terms. However, the development of relevant price deflators will also be reviewed briefly, if they show market changes in various phases of monetary policy.

While divergent views still exist on the detail of the transmission process of monetary policy, at the level of general description there appear to be three important elements in the process by which financial factors affect the real economy.

Cost-of-Capital Effects

The working of this transmission process depends on the existence of money and capital markets where prices, i.e. interest rates, on marketable liabilities and assets adjust very rapidly to excess demand or supply situations. With the expected yield on a unit of real capital initially stable, the rise in interest rates on financial assets and in the cost of borrowing funds will lead to the purchase of existing financial assets and the reduction of new debt to acquire real capital. This will reduce the price of existing units of real capital relative to the cost of producing new units, and narrow or possibly reverse any initial gap between desired and actual stocks of capital with the possible result of slowdowns in the production of new capital goods. This channel could operate on the demands for both business and consumer capital — including plant and equipment, inventories, residential construction, and consumer durable goods.

Credit Availability Effects

In an economy where a rigid set of institutional arrangements does not allow a quick adjustment of the prices of marketable assets and liabilities to excess demand or supply situations in the money and capital markets, the channel of monetary policy described above will not work well. In such a system, in any relatively short period of time the observed levels of interest rates are not simultaneously on the supply curves of lenders and the demand curves of borrowers; the demand for credit is limited not by the borrower's willingness to borrow at the given rate, but by the lender's willingness to lend. This implies that monetary policy would affect expenditures by changing the financial institutions' capacity or willingness to lend, even if monetary controls did not change interest rates appreciably or if aggregate demand were interest inelastic. The importance of credit availability effects on various categories of expenditures may differ according to the degree of dependence on external funds in financing these expenditures.

Wealth Effects

A restrictive monetary policy raises the capitalization rates used in the evaluation of expected income flows, and reduces the market value of outstanding bonds, real wealth and equity claims thereto. The decline in the valuation of corporate assets may have deflationary effects on business investment, reinforcing portfolio adjustment through cost-of-capital effects described earlier. In addition, in an economy where the household sector holds bonds and other assets, the decline in the value of these assets may have a contractionary impact on consumption. However, the importance of such effects will depend not only on the size of security holdings but also on the time horizon in determining consumption. While a rise in bond yields leads to a capital loss now, the holder of bonds will have a rise in income at some time in the future when he will refund at a more favourable interest rate (if interest rates do not change). Therefore, he may not change his spending pattern significantly. Somewhat similar arguments can be applied to the effect on consumption of the decline in stock prices: households who can buy stocks hereafter at a lower cost per unit of return in continuing their financial investment may reduce their saving ratios, rather than raise them.

The importance of various sectoral effects, the length and variability of time lags, and the specification of financial variables directly related to expenditures are essentially empirical rather than theoretical issues. Answers to these questions will diverge according to countries, reflecting the difference in the structure of the real and financial economy and the choice of monetary instruments discussed in Parts I and II. Accordingly, the following review of the role of financial factors in the determination of the level of economic activity is based on a country-by-country analysis, and the result of the Secretariat's and other econometric work will be examined in the context of basic institutional factors.

a) *Non-residential fixed investment*

In the *United States,* there is relatively firm evidence of the effects of monetary policy on non-residential fixed investment (Chart 30). Upswings in this type of investment occurred at a late stage of each of the two expansionary phases (1960–62 and 1970–71). On the first occasion, a decline at an annual rate of 4 per cent during the first four quarters after the introduction of expansionary monetary policy was followed by an increase at an annual rate of 7 per cent in the subsequent quarters up to the end of that period; during the second expansionary phase, a fall at an annual rate of about 8 per cent during the first year was matched by the subsequent pick-up at a similar rate. The pattern of the response points to a long lag in the effect of monetary policy on non-residential fixed investment. In fact, during the two short periods of restraint (the fourth quarter of 1965 to the third quarter of 1966, and the fourth quarter of 1968 to the fourth quarter of 1969), there was no noticeable deceleration; the annual rate of change from the beginning to the end of the first and second restrictive phases was 7.3 per cent and 6.7 per cent respectively. This virtually identical development corresponded to a broadly similar pattern of response of interest rates in the two periods.

A number of econometric studies provide information on the role of various financial variables in the determination of non-residential fixed investment in the United States. Most of the evidence is from single-equation studies of the determinants of corporate behaviour.[1] A series of studies by Jorgenson and associates suggests that interest rates have an important influence on investment behaviour, while availability effects are of little significance. They also indicate that the response of investment is rather slow with a peak somewhere between 6 and 12 quarters. These findings are generally supported by the results of other time-series studies. Various cross-section studies generally also find a dominant role of a cost-of-capital effect with a long lag, although one major investigator admits the existence of effects on corporate investment from reduced availability of bank loans during the monetary restraint of 1966.

Large-scale econometric models so far developed in the United States have had little to add to what emerges from the single-equation invest-

1. The evidence is surveyed in G. Fisher and D. Sheppard, "Effects of Monetary Policy on the United States Economy, A Survey of Econometric Evidence", *OECD Economic Outlook. Occasional Studies*, December 1972, Chapter 2. References to the voluminous literature can also be found there.

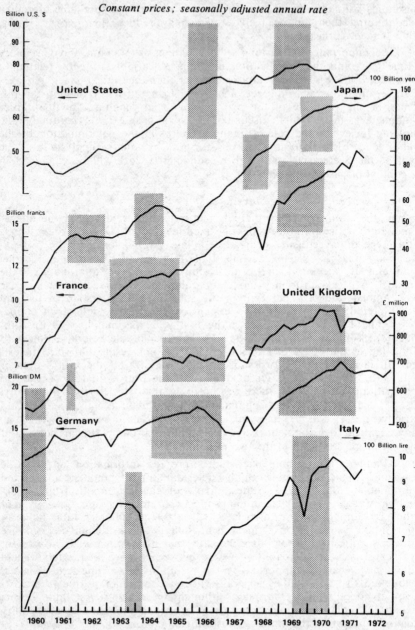

Chart 30. PRIVATE NON-RESIDENTIAL FIXED INVESTMENT
Constant prices; seasonally adjusted annual rate

ment studies.[1] The FMP model (see page 79) incorporates only a cost-of-capital effect. The pattern of the response of investment to monetary policy changes may be most clearly indicated by partial simulations

1. *Ibid.*, and OECD Monetary Studies Series, *Monetary Policy in the United States*, Part III.

which illustrate the direct impact of financial variables, ignoring the structural relations within the real sector and the feed-back to the financial sector; the calculations should, therefore, be compared with the results of single-equation studies which measure only the direct financial impact on demand. They suggest that a 50 basis-point increase in the Treasury Bill rate from the end of 1968 would have induced a decline in private fixed non-residential investment of the order of 0.4 per cent at the end of four quarters, and about 1 per cent in six quarters (Table 2). The effect shows no sign of tapering off towards the end of the 12-quarter period covered by the simulation. The full simulation, where multiplier, accelerator and other effects inside the real sector are allowed to work their way through, more than doubles the size of the response, but the time pattern remains the same.

In *Japan,* private non-residential fixed investment has been a volatile demand component, and its adjustment has been an important objective of the authorities. The response of this investment to changes in monetary policy has been remarkable, notably in the restrictive periods of the 1960s (Chart 30). In the first period of restraint (July 1961 to October 1962) private non-residential capital formation started to follow a decline two quarters after that policy step; in the second period (end-1963 to end-1964), the lag was about three quarters. In the third restrictive period (September 1967 to August 1968), investment expenditure showed a deceleration about two quarters after the first action of monetary restraint, and then reaccelerated as export market conditions improved and the stance of monetary policy became less restrictive. In the fourth restrictive period (September 1969 to October 1970), expenditure started to decelerate again about two quarters after the first measures of restraint. An increase in investment followed the adoption of an expansionary policy, but the length of the lag was somewhat more variable. While investment started to pick up about two quarters after the initial action of monetary ease taken in the fourth quarter of 1962, the lag was about four quarters in the two expansionary phases following the second and fourth restrictive periods. The delayed response largely reflected the high level of capital stock accumulated during the preceding long investment booms and enterprises' pessimistic views on the future course of the economy. There was no noticeable cyclical change in investment in the period following the third restrictive phase, and this was consistent with the stance of policy which was then neutral rather than reflationary.

The OECD Secretariat's single-equation study[1] finds that changes in credit availability affect fixed investment significantly with a relatively short lag. Quarterly equations suggest that both the increase in domestic bank credit to the private sector in the current and previous three quarters and the increase in total external funds raised by the corporate sector with the same lag pattern are highly significant in explaining private non-residential fixed investment. In the Secretariat's half-yearly model for the Japanese economy, the equation for private productive capital formation includes, as a significant explanatory variable, increases in domestic bank credit to the private sector in the current and the previous half-years. For the purpose of measuring the direct and indirect impacts of monetary policy on this demand component (as well as other expenditure variables to be reviewed later), it is possible to use this model which takes into account the inter-

---

1. OECD Monetary Studies Series, *Monetary Policy in Japan,* pp. 101-103.

dependence within the real sector, while treating domestic bank credit as determined solely by monetary policy[1] and thus disregarding the feedback to this variable from the real sector. A simulation was run in which it was assumed that bank credit expansion accelerated in the first half of 1969 to such an extent as to raise its year-to-year growth rate at mid-1969 by one percentage point (to 16.7 per cent from the actual rate of 15.7 per cent) and thereafter followed the same course as actually observed. The result suggests that the associated percentage increase in private productive capital investment is of the order of 1.6 in the first half-year, reaching a peak of 3.7 in the second half-year and diminishing in the subsequent periods (Table 3). Though these numerical results are of a preliminary nature, they clearly indicate the importance of the availability effect on this type of demand.

In *Germany* also, there were clear downswings in business productive investment activity in restrictive periods (Chart 30). In one such phase, starting in mid-1964, a sharp declining trend began about 6 quarters after the introduction of restrictive policy. In the restrictive period of 1969–1971, a fall in the level of investment set in about 8 quarters after the initial action of restraint. The apparent longer lag seems to have been related to the distortion of companies' reports on quarterly investment figures as a result of the effect of short-lived tax measures on their expenditures. There is some econometric evidence that business equipment investment has been influenced by changes in the cost of borrowing rather than credit availability effects. Rosette[2] found that market interest rates are useful variables in explaining German industries' investment activity. The OECD Secretariat's econometric work[3] also points to a significant role of real bond yields in the determination of private non-residential fixed investment. Though the issuance of bonds is a minor source of corporations' external funds, bond yields can be used as an approximation for their average cost of borrowing, since the term structure of German interest rates has been stable (page 76). The result of this single-equation analysis is incorporated into the OECD Secretariat's preliminary quarterly model for the German economy. The simulation of one half percentage point increase in bond yields above the actual path from the first quarter of 1969 onwards suggests that, *ceteris paribus,* the associated percentage decline in this demand component is virtually nil up to the second quarter, about 2 in the fourth quarter and reaches a peak of about 2.7 around the sixth quarter, with the impact gradually diminishing thereafter (Table 4).

Italy is another country which experienced a sharp fall in business non-residential fixed investment in the two restrictive periods of the 1960s (Chart 30).[4] In fact, investment in machinery and equipment levelled off in the third quarter of 1963 when restrictive monetary policy was introduced and it declined sharply between the first quarter of 1964 and the first quarter of the following year; the mid-1969 tightening of monetary policy was followed by a marked decline in machinery and equipment investment

---

1. This assumption seems appropriate at least in the restrictive periods when major banks closely observed credit ceilings imposed upon them, and other banks' credit expansion also showed the same pattern (OECD Monetary Studies Series, *Monetary Policy in Japan,* **Appendix III,** Section II).
2. Joachim Rosette, "Oekonometrische Investitionsfunktionen für Konjunkturmodelle", *Konjunkturpolitik,* 1971, III.
3. OECD Monetary Studies Series, *Monetary Policy in Germany,* p. 82.
4. OECD Monetary Studies Series, *Monetary Policy in Italy,* Part IV.

during the second half of the year. However, in the case of Italy, the role of monetary policy in bringing about these remarkable declines in investment does not seem to have been significant. On the first occasion, the fact that a deceleration of monetary expansion set in before the introduction of restrictive monetary policy and without any noticeable rise in market interest rates suggests that the downturn in business investment was caused primarily by autonomous factors. The decline in the second half of 1969 was mainly due to unsettled labour market situations leading to widespread strikes late in the year, while other downswings from the beginning of 1971 seem too sharp to be explained as a lagged reaction to the moderately restrictive monetary policy in use until the third quarter of 1970.

There is no strong evidence about the effects of changes in financial conditions on total private productive investment or on its main identifiable components (on an annual basis) by sectors. In a quarterly econometric model developed by the University of Bologna no financial variables enter in the equation for investment in machinery and transportation equipment. On the other hand, the Bank of Italy's econometric findings based on annual data using a somewhat different breakdown of investment[1] provide some evidence of a cost-of-capital effect on industrial fixed non-residential investment; a percentage point increase in the long-term bond rate was related towards the end of the 1960s to a decline of industrial investment by 60-70 billion lire in the course of a year. This represents a very small impact compared with the total magnitude of such spending, which amounted to 4,000 billion lire (1963 prices) towards the end of the 1960s. The study has also identified the existence of a cost-of-capital effect on fixed investment by the services sector, but the size of the coefficient for this variable is about one-tenth of that for industrial investment, suggesting that the effect is virtually negligible.

While the countries examined above have experienced declines in the level of investment activity in at least some restrictive periods, *France* has had only one such experience caused by the general strike in the second quarter of 1968 (Chart 30). Nevertheless, it is possible to observe that in each of the two restrictive periods (the first quarter 1963 to mid-1965, and the fourth quarter 1968 to mid-1970), there was a deceleration in investment activity. Deceleration was more moderate in the second period when the authorities fixed separate, less tight, ceilings on credit to finance productive investment while applying stringent quantitative controls to short-term and non-priority longer-term credits. The development of investment in easy money periods was irregular. This suggests that non-monetary factors such as capacity utilization ratios and order inflows played dominant roles in the determination of investment in such periods. In addition, fiscal measures seem to have influenced business investment activity in the second reflationary phase.

The OECD Secretariat has tested the effect of financial variables on plant and equipment investment and found that this demand component is closely related to interest rates on bank lending (adjusted for price increases) lagged two quarters and to bank credit expansion during the current and previous quarters, as well as real variables such as profit

---

1. The main references are *Un Modello Econometrico dell'Economia Italiana (M1, B1), Settore Reale e Fiscale*, Bank of Italy, January 1970, and " Project Link, a Quarterly Econometric Model of the Italian Economy", *Discussion Paper*, No. 7203, April 1973, Istituto di Scienze Economiche, University of Bologna, and mimeographed notes on the real model (M1, B1, RF4) from the Bank of Italy (1972).

margins, capacity utilization ratios and relative costs of productive factors. The equations suggest that the fall in capital formation associated with a one per cent reduction in bank credit and a percentage point increase in interest rates is of the order of 0.4 per cent and 0.2 per cent respectively.[1]

In the *United Kingdom,* there has been no visually clear correspondence between changes in the stance of monetary policy and the investment cycles which occur mainly in manufacturing industry (Chart 30). Productive capital formation rose during the first period of restraint (January-October 1960) and the subsequent period of monetary ease. The Central Statistical Office finds an upper turning point in the third quarter of 1961 which roughly corresponds with the second, albeit short-lived period of monetary restraint (July-October 1961). Investment started to pick up in the second quarter of 1963, near the middle of the following easy period and reached a new peak towards the end of 1965, about 4 quarters after the beginning of the third restrictive period. A rise in the initial stage of the subsequent short period of ease was soon reversed to hit a trough in the autumn of 1967 when the fourth period of monetary restriction started. Investment maintained an upward trend until late 1970, but dropped sharply in the first quarter of 1971. In the subsequent period of monetary relaxation starting in the spring of that year, investment activity remained weak until late 1972.

Although these visual observations are difficult to interpret, there are some econometric studies which suggest the existence of interest rate effects on private non-residential capital formation. Hines and Catephores[2] found that manufacturing investment was significantly related to interest rates with a lag of six quarters. Nobay's econometric study[3] shows that the fit of investment functions is in some cases improved by the inclusion of a cost-of-capital variable with a lag of five quarters. But its significance varied according to the other explanatory variables used in the functions. The Treasury's unpublished work also reached somewhat similar conclusions. On the other hand, Goodhart of the Bank of England[4] used bank lending to the private sector and a long-term rate as explanatory variables in investment functions and found that both had the wrong sign.

b) *Inventory investment*

In *Japan,* inventory investment has been the most volatile demand component, and its stabilization has constituted an important objective of monetary policy. The response of this type of demand to monetary policy changes was notably quick (with a lag of one to two quarters) and strong in the first two periods of restraint and in the intervening period of monetary ease (Chart 31). In the second phase of monetary ease, a similarly quick upturn occurred, but it was soon interrupted by the unexpectedly weak response of final demand; recovery set in only about four quarters after the introduction of easy monetary policy. In the subsequent period

1.   OECD Monetary Studies Series, *Monetary Policy in France*, Part IV.C.
2.   A.G. Hines and G. Catephores, "Investment in U.K. Manufacturing Industry, 1956–1967", in D.F. Heathfield and K. Hilton (eds.), *The Econometric Study of the U.K.*, 1970.
3.   A.R. Nobay, " Forecasting Manufacturing Investment – Some Preliminary Results ", *National Institute Economic Review*, May 1970.
4.   C.A.E. Goodhart, "The Transmission Mechanism of Monetary Policy" *unpublished* paper presented at the Konstanz monetary seminar, June 1971.

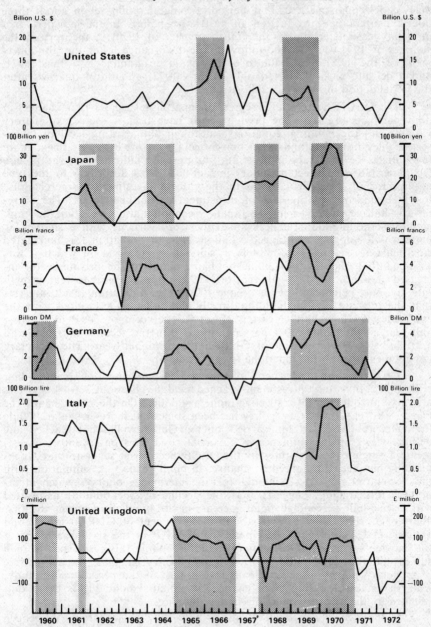

of monetary restriction, the deceleration again began promptly. But the extent of the slowdown was moderate, reflecting a quick improvement of export prospects and the subsequent less restrictive stance of policy. In the following period of monetary neutrality, inventory accumulation was distorted by unusual weather conditions, and the resulting relatively low level of stocks at the beginning of the following period of restraint tended to delay stock adjustment in that period: the deceleration set in about three quarters after the introduction of restrictive policy. In the last period of monetary ease (starting in the fourth quarter of 1970), a recovery in the summer of 1971 was reversed following the disturbances after the announcement of the U.S. new balance of payments programme in August 1971, and a definite pick-up started only in early 1972, about five quarters after the initial action of monetary relaxation.

The OECD Secretariat's regression analysis[1] suggests that changes in domestic bank credit to the private sector have been a useful explanatory variable in stockbuilding equations, although the existing level of inventories, sales prospects and other non-monetary factors have, at times, more than offset the monetary impact. Its findings also indicate that the precise lag pattern of the direct monetary impact has varied according to the type of inventories: from virtually nil in the case of investment in merchandise to three quarters in the case of investment in finished goods. The Secretariat's half-yearly model for the Japanese economy also uses domestic bank credit to the private sector as an explanatory variable with a similar lag pattern (with no lag and lagged a half-year) in the equation for aggregated stockbuilding. Using this model, a simulation was run in which it was assumed that the flow of domestic bank credit to the private sector increased enough in the first half-year of 1969 to raise the year-to-year growth rate by one percentage point (page 102). The simulation result suggests that the increase in stockbuilding directly and indirectly associated with the assumed growth in bank credit is about 0.3 per cent of GNP in the first half-year, slightly above 0.4 per cent of GNP in the second half-year, and a little below 0.3 per cent of GNP in the third half-year. The monetary impact dies down in the fourth half-year (Table 3).

Germany also experienced a clear cyclical movement of stockbuilding (Chart 31). Inventory investment reached peak levels about 2 to 4 quarters after the introduction of restrictive monetary policy. On the other hand, the response to easy monetary policy has been somewhat more irregular. While the empirical work so far carried out in Germany has not reached any definite views on the influence of financial conditions on inventory investment, a single-equation study by the OECD Secretariat suggests that stockbuilding has been influenced by changes in bond yields.[2] A simulation with the Secretariat's quarterly model for the German economy, which incorporates this finding, suggests that the decline in stockbuilding associated with a one-half percentage point increase in real bond yields from the first quarter of 1969 onwards is about 0.1 per cent of GNP in the second quarter, and slightly above 0.2 per cent of GNP in the sixth quarter, with the impact tapering off thereafter (Table 4). While this result points to a susceptibility of stockbuilding to monetary policy changes, the actual role of monetary policy has been small during most of the period under study, with the stabilizing impact of changes in nominal bond yields being outweighed by the contrary effect of changes in prices.

In the *United Kingdom*, inventory cycles, which are largely influenced by changes in manufacturing industries' stocks and work in progress, have been somewhat more irregular (Chart 31). Stock accumulation reached the

---

1. OECD Monetary Studies Series, *Monetary Policy in Japan*, pp. 97-101.
2. See below for the use of bond yields as an approximation for the average cost of corporate borrowing.

first peak about two quarters after the introduction of monetary restraint in 1960, and thereafter continued to decelerate through the subsequent period of ease and the second period of restraint to reach a trough around end-1962 (about five quarters after the start of the second expansionary policy phase). The second peak coincided with the introduction of restrictive monetary policy towards the end of 1964, and investment continued to decelerate through this restrictive period and the subsequent short period of relaxation. It began to show a definite sign of recovery in the early part of the fourth restrictive period (introduced in the autumn of 1967), and a deceleration started only about 6 quarters after the introduction of that policy. In the following period of monetary expansion, inventories followed the declining trend until the end of 1972.

There has been no econometric work so far carried out in the United Kingdom which points to a significant role of interest rates in the determination of stock accumulation over short periods. A study by Trivedi[1] suggests that a rise in interest rates reduces the level of stocks which manufacturers desire to hold, but the actual reduction in stocks is spread over a long period. On the other hand, Goodhart[2] found that the short-term rate (local authority rate) lagged one quarter had a negative but not significant coefficient; the same rate lagged two quarters also included in the equation had a positive coefficient. Similar results were obtained using a two-stage estimation technique.

In *France,* the introduction of restrictive monetary policy was followed by a deceleration in stockbuilding. The lag between the initial action of monetary restraint and the slowdown in inventory investment was about 4 quarters in the first episode and about 3 quarters in the second. In the intervening period of expansionary monetary policy, the recovery in stockbuilding was rapid and strong. On the other hand, during the first and third periods of monetary ease, there was no noticeable acceleration of inventory accumulation (Chart 31).

There has apparently been no econometric work other than that of the OECD Secretariat to examine the role of financial variables in the determination of inventory investment in France. According to the Secretariat's analysis,[3] both bank credit expansion during the current and preceding quarters and the change in the real cost of bank borrowing (nominal cost adjusted for price changes) play certain roles in explaining inventory investment. But the significance of these variables differs greatly, depending on the formulation of inventory equations and the combination of the explanatory variables. The preliminary conclusion is that the direct effect of financial variables on inventory investment is relatively small and that monetary policy affects this type of investment mainly indirectly through influencing final demand. In fact, real variables related to corporate sales, capacity utilization ratios and profits are very significant explanatory variables in the Secretariat's equations for inventory investment.

In the *United States,* the development of inventory investment varied between the first and second period of monetary expansion (Chart 31). In contrast to the first period (1960–62) when the reversal of the deceleration in inventory investment took place only in the second year, the accumulation

1. P.K. Trivedi, "Inventory Behaviour in U.K. Manufacturing 1956–1967", *Review of Economic Studies,* October 1970.
2. *Op. cit.*
3. OECD Monetary Studies Series, *Monetary Policy in France,* Part IV.C.

of stocks started to accelerate immediately after the introduction of easy policy on the second occasion (1970–71). There was also a difference in the pattern of stockbuilding between the first and second periods of restraint (fourth quarter 1965 to third quarter 1966, and fourth quarter 1968 to fourth quarter 1969). Though it weakened in the second period, it continued to follow the rising trend in the first period. The strength of stock accumulation in the first restrictive period was related at least partly to a rapid military build-up as a result of the escalation of the Vietnam War.

Time series studies in the United States have found little evidence of direct cost effects on inventory accumulation.[1] This may be due in part to the difficulty of distinguishing between planned and unplanned stock changes; observed changes in inventories are often a poor proxy for the former. A large cross-section study has assessed the response of non-farm inventory investment to the monetary stringency in 1966–67. This study suggests a reduction of intended inventory accumulation by about 3.50 per cent in 1966, mainly in the second half of the year, and a rather larger decline in 1967. The lags involved are rather long, and it may be the expectational rather than the cost or availability elements which are important; on this interpretation, the high correlation observable between inventory investment and bank loans is not attributable to a causal link through availability effects. This does not of course mean that monetary policy has no influence on inventory investment. In fact this category of demand depends strongly on other demand components which are sensitive to changes in financial variables, and it is thus influenced indirectly by monetary policy. The full simulation of the FMP model (page 100) suggests that the changes in inventory investment associated with a 50 basis-point change in the Treasury bill rate is of the order of 0.13 per cent of GNF at the end of four quarters and 0.3 per cent of GNP after eight quarters (Table 2).

In *Italy,* it is possible to observe turning points in the quarterly estimates of stockbuilding provided by the University of Bologna[2] (Chart 31). In the first period of monetary restraint (third quarter 1963 to first quarter 1964) inventory investment started to decelerate relatively quickly (about two quarters) after the introduction of restrictive policy. In the subsequent easy period, it remained flat throughout 1964 and picked up in early 1965. Stock accumulation levelled off in the latter half of the second restrictive period (mid-1969 to third quarter 1970). In the following period of expansionary policy, a sharp deceleration in the first quarter of 1971 was followed by a levelling in the subsequent quarters. While these visual observations point to a susceptibility of stockbuilding to monetary influences, there has been, so far, no firm econometric evidence about the effect of monetary policy on this type of investment in Italy.

c) *Residential construction*

In the *United States,* residential construction has moved fairly closely in line with the development of monetary conditions, although with some lag (Chart 32). During the first period of monetary expansion (1960–62) investment initially declined and then rose beginning in 1961. In the second period of monetary ease (1970–71), housing starts turned up in March 1970, and expenditures recovered strongly from the third quarter of that

1. See Fisher and Sheppard, *op. cit.*, and the references given there.
2. In the official national accounts, inventory investment is not separable from private consumption.

year. Residential expenditure fell in the two periods of monetary restraint (1966 and 1969). The magnitude of the decline was smaller in 1969, largely reflecting the intervention of the Federal government in the housing market. In view of the experience in the year 1966, when monetary restriction hit the housing sector more severely than was desirable on social grounds, the authorities stepped up Federal lending to housebuilders in 1969 to offset part of the restrictive impact of monetary policy on the housing market.

There is relatively firm econometric evidence of a quick and strong effect of monetary policy changes on residential investment expenditure, and both cost and availability variables appear to play important roles in the equations for housing starts (the elasticity of starts with respect to mortgage rates is estimated to be larger than minus one-half in several studies, and the average lag in the response is between one and two quarters, considerably shorter than those for spending on consumer durables and productive investment (see pages 99 and 114). Since the lag between housing starts and expenditure is rather short, the impact of monetary policy is also considered to be quickly transmitted to residential investment spending. The partial simulation of the FMF model suggests that the change of housing investment associated with a 50 basis-point change in the Treasury bill rate is slightly below 1 per cent at the end of the fourth quarter, 1.4 per cent in the eighth quarter and 1.6 per cent in the tenth quarter (Table 2). The impact measured by the full simulation for the respective quarters are about 2.4, 4.7 and 5.1 per cent. These results represent, a combination of a cost-of-capital effect and an availability effect. Up to the eighth quarter, the latter effect accounts for slightly more than half of the total response; subsequently its relative importance declines. This pattern is consistent with the behaviour of savings and loan associations and mutual savings banks which adopt more competitive rates with a fairly long lag and gradually adjust their unfavourable position in competing with commercial banks for deposits (see page 82).

The *United Kingdom* has also experienced clear housing cycles (Chart 32). Private residential construction levelled off in the second half of the first restrictive period. It accelerated in the following period of monetary ease, reaching a peak towards the end of the second, short-lived, period of monetary restraint. In the initial stage of the easy monetary period starting in late 1961, the volume of housing construction declined, while the cost of construction rose sharply (5 per cent in 1962 against 1.50 per cent in the previous year), and it was only around mid-1963 that the volume began to increase strongly. The recovery was reversed soon after the start of the third restrictive period. It revived quickly and sharply in the subsequent short period of monetary ease in 1967 and slowed down immediately following the reimposition of restrictive monetary measures late that year. The upturn started promptly after the recovery of the building societies' financial position which resulted from the downward adjustment of the bank rate in the spring of 1970. Thus the conclusion reached by Vipond[1] through turning-point analysis which indicates the strong sensitivity of housing investment to credit conditions during the period 1950–1966 also seems valid for the more recent period. The cost of construction rose sharply in 1971 and 1972 (about 8 and 8.50 per cent respectively), which also tends to confirm the earlier impression that, at least in the upswing, much of the monetary effect comes on prices.

1. M.J. Vipond, "Fluctuations in Private Housebuilding in Great Britain, 1950–1966", *Scottish Journal of Political Economy*, June 1969.

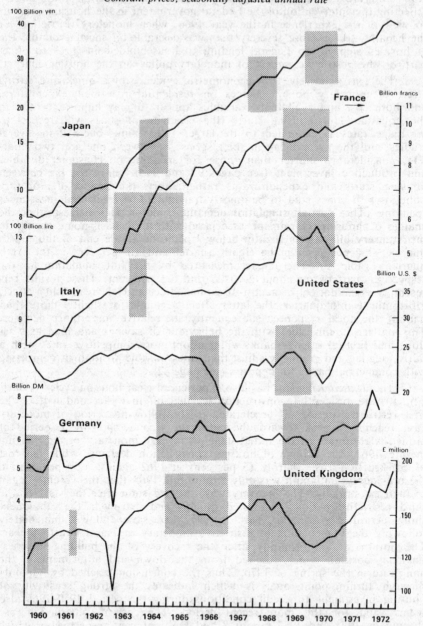

Chart 32. PRIVATE RESIDENTIAL CONSTRUCTION

Constant prices, seasonally adjusted annual rate

In the United Kingdom a large part (about two-thirds) of house purchases is made on credit supplied by building societies. Not only variations in the cost of borrowing but also changes in the availability of such credit have an important influence on housing investment. These institutions closely follow the Building Societies Association's recommended rates on loans and deposits, which tend to be sticky partly because of political considerations.[1] This relationship has resulted in a sharp decline in the inflow of funds to the building societies when competing interest rates have risen following increases in Bank rate and the societies have had to ration home loans at the recommended rate. The role of the availability effect as well as the cost effect is confirmed by a recent study by Goodhart.[2] His housing expenditure equation includes, as significant explanatory variables, both the short-term rate (local authority rate) and the difference between the short rate and the Building Societies Association's recommended rate on deposits. The former variable is used to represent the general level of interest rates, and the latter to pick up the availability of loanable funds at the building societies. Both effects appear after the second quarter and continue through six quarters. A study by Whitehead[3] which explains the demand and supply of private housing completions in both equilibrium and disequilibrium conditions suggests that changes in the long-term rate influence completions with a distribution lag of one to several quarters.

In *Italy*, visual observation of the course of housing construction points to the susceptibility of this demand component to monetary policy changes (Chart 32). During the first period of restraint (third quarter 1963 to first quarter 1964), housing construction continued to rise in the first two quarters and then levelled off. In the subsequent period of reflationary monetary policy (second quarter 1964 to mid-1969) a moderate decline stopped towards the end of 1964. It started to rise in early 1967, about 11 quarters after the initial action of monetary ease. Residential investment fell erratically from the second quarter of 1969 before the beginning of the second period of moderate monetary restraint (mid-1969 to third quarter 1970). A substantial fall started in the first half of 1970, and it continued during the first three quarters of the subsequent reflationary period.

According to the annual econometric model of the Bank of Italy (page 103), the only financial variable which has a meaningful correlation with housing expenditure is credit flow from financial institutions specialized in mortgage finance. However, this variable, which is used without lag, represents only about half of the external finance or about 20 per cent of total funds for housing, so it is not clear whether the variable picks up the availability effect. Two other financial variables used without lag in the Bank of Italy's equations (mortgage rates and changes in the general public's holdings of fixed interest-rate securities) have coefficients with the "wrong" signs (positive for the former and negative for the latter). On the other hand, changes in the long-term bond rate are used as a significant explanatory variable with a distributed lag of one to eight quarters in the University of Bologna's quarterly equation for residential and industrial construction. This equation suggests that a little more than half of the total impact of a percentage increase in the long rate on this category of investment is felt during the first year, corresponding to about 1.5 per cent of annual investment. However, the actual changes in the long rate were not large enough to explain the weakening in construction in the 1964 recession and a sharper decline in 1970-71.

1. For example, in 1965 the government asked the Association not to raise interest rates. Recently the stickiness of mortgage and deposit rates has resulted in a very small inflow of funds, necessitating a government loan to the societies to supplement their resources.
2. *Op. cit.*
3. C. Whitehead, "A Model of the U.K. Housing Market", *Bulletin of Oxford University Institute of Economics and Statistics*, November 1971.

In *France,* government-subsidized ("aided") residential investment is largely financed by a public credit institution (Crédit Foncier). Bank credit is only a supplementary source of finance for this type of housing construction, and the public institution's prior approval for its credit extension is considered to be the major determinant. On the other hand, "non-aided" housing investment is largely financed by bank credit. Turning-point analysis conveys the impression that the development of housing starts in the "non-aided" sector was at times influenced largely by changes in monetary conditions. Unfortunately, disaggregation into the two types of housing construction is possible on the basis of starts but not on that of expenditure. Chart 32 shows total housing construction. While starts continued to rise sharply throughout the restrictive period of 1963 to mid-1965, reflecting strong housing demand by repatriates from Algeria, the slowdown set in about two quarters after the tightening of monetary policy in the restrictive period of 1969 to mid-1970. The recovery in the subsequent period was delayed by the large stock of unsold houses accumulated towards the end of the preceding restrictive period. On the other hand, expansionary monetary policy introduced in the second half of 1968 was quickly followed by an acceleration in housing starts for the "non-aided" sector.

Unpublished work at the Bank of France suggests a close inverse relationship between annual housing starts and the interest rate on banks' housing loans in the current year. Three other financial variables were used, also without lag: yields on bonds and shares (with a negative sign), the maximum term of banks' housing credit (with a positive sign) and house developers' borrowings outstanding at the beginning of the current year (with a negative sign). The negative coefficient for the last variable is interpreted by the Bank of France to indicate that the investment incentive for house developers will tend to weaken as their outstanding borrowings rise.

Japan has not experienced cyclical changes in housing construction as clearly as the four countries already discussed. Even so, residential investment has always shown some deceleration in periods of monetary restriction and acceleration in those of monetary ease (Chart 32). Econometric studies covering the period up to the end of the 1960s did not definitely point to the existence of a direct monetary influence on residential construction. The equation for this demand component in the Bank of Japan's comprehensive model[1] does not include any financial variables. The OECD Secretariat's single-equation analysis[2] over the period up to the first quarter of 1970 shows a close correlation between residential investment and the money stock held by the personal sector (adjusted for price changes and lagged two quarters). But when personal disposable income is introduced as another variable in the equation, the explanatory power of the financial variable becomes insignificant, suggesting that its impact may simply reflect that of income rather than the real balance (or wealth) effect. Interest rates and other financial variables also prove insignificant for that period, and the development of residential construction is explained by the initial stock of houses, personal disposable income, and the prices of houses relative to those of consumer goods. Monetary policy is considered to have affected

1. "The Bank of Japan Econometric Model", Bank of Japan, *Monthly Economic Review,* (in Japanese), September 1972.
2. OECD Monetary Studies Series, *Monetary Policy in Japan,* p. 104.

construction indirectly through an influence on the compensation of employees and on the income of unincorporated enterprises, which are the main sources of personal income.

The OECD Secretariat's half-yearly model for the Japanese economy, which includes no financial variables in the housing equation, can be used at least to take rough measurement of the indirect monetary influence on private housing construction. The result of the simulation of an increase in the flow of bank credit in the first-half of 1969 equivalent to a one percentage point rise in its year-to-year growth rate at mid-1969 (page 102) shows that the associated percentage change in private housing construction is 0.2 in the first half-year (Table 3). Although the percentage change more than doubles in the subsequent three half-years, it is still considerably smaller than the impact on private non-residential fixed investment already reviewed. A more recent single-equation study by the Bank of Japan [1] suggests that the flow of private financial institutions' housing loans (lagged one quarter) is a useful financial variable in explaining the development of housing investment in the years 1970-72. The study also confirms the earlier view that direct monetary influences were negligible in the 1960s. The significance of housing loans in the more recent period seems to reflect the growing importance of external funds in financing housing investment.

In *Germany,* housing construction has been the most stable demand component (Chart 32), and it is difficult to detect any relationship between its development and changes in key financial variables. There is no econometric analysis which provides evidence that credit availability affects this demand component. In fact, the building and loans associations' intermediate credit accelerated in most restrictive periods when longer-term housing credit by mortgage banks and savings banks tended to decelerate. The total availability of funds for housing finance and therefore housing expenditure would, therefore, not have been affected significantly by monetary policy changes, even though the former type of credit is not a perfect substitute for the latter.

Some attempts have been made in Germany to relate the development of private housing construction with interest rate changes. For example, a study by Nullau [2] covering the period 1954-1964 suggests that a rise in interest rates was generally followed by a slowdown in housing investment with a lag of about half a year, while the recovery of this type of investment tended to lag behind a fall in interest rates by about a year. It was also found that the interest sensitivity increases in line with the extent of interest rate changes, and that a variation of less than a percentage point has little impact on the investment activity. His findings have, however, failed to explain the development of private housing construction in the subsequent periods of monetary ease and restriction. A noticeable rise in interest rates starting in the first quarter of 1965 was followed by a weakening of housing construction which set in only around mid-1966. Though the effect of a decline in interest rates in the subsequent period of monetary ease (starting in late 1966) appears to support his finding of a one-year lag in the transmission of the effect of interest rate changes, the recovery coincided with the introduction of specific policy

1. " Consumer Credit by Japanese Financial Institutions ", Bank of Japan, *Monthly Economic Review*, (in Japanese), August 1973.
2. Bruno Nullau, " Die Wirkungsverzögerungen bei der Finanzierung von Investitionen im Wohnungsbau ", *Sonderhefte des DIW*, No. 79, Berlin 1968.

113

programmes to encourage housebuilding (including subsidies to private house developers), and the general view is that these measures played the dominant role in the recovery.

Housing construction remained strong throughout the restrictive period of early 1969 to mid-1971. It started to show a definite sign of slowdown near the end of 1972, about a year after interest rates resumed the rising trend. Although the above observation of turning points does not negate the susceptibility of private housebuilding to interest rate changes, no firm econometric evidence has yet established a close and stable relationship between the two variables; nor has the importance of interest rates relative to other factors such as personal disposable income, public subsidies and price expectations been clarified.[1]

d) *Consumption*

In the *United States,* there were clear cyclical movements of private consumption, notably durables (Chart 33). A reversal of the course of expenditure on durables occurred in the later stages of each of the two expansionary periods (1960-62 and 1970-71), while expenditure on non-durables remained stable. On the first occasion, a small decline (1.6 per cent) of consumption on durables in the first year was followed by a strong rise (6.4 per cent per year) in the subsequent two years; during the second period, a fall (9 per cent) in the first year was reversed by a sharp rise (21 per cent) in the subsequent year. During the two short periods of restraint in 1966 and 1969, the growth of consumption of durables was lower than the rate for the previous year and lower than its long-term trend.

A number of econometric studies find an effect from interest rate changes on consumer durables. However, some of them do not use the market value of net worth, so the interest rate term must be regarded as reflecting both cost-of-borrowing and wealth effects. One important study[2] includes a measure of the real value of household liquidity (M2 plus deposits with non-bank financial institutions), which represents the ability to make initial payments and, presumably, the availability of institutional finance. The discrete time lag in the impact of interest rates (measured as the corporate Aaa bond rate) is generally 4-5 quarters for automobiles and 6 quarters for other durables. Since rates on consumer finance tend to lag bond rates in the cycle, this finding suggests that the lag between changes in consumer credit terms and changes in consumer durables is shorter, with a peak occurring after 2-4 quarters. The calculated interest elasticities are close to -.9 for automobiles and -.7 for other durables. Thus this study gives evidence of a significant response of durable expenditures to cost or wealth effects. Studies by Branson and Klevorick[3] and Modigliani[4] suggest

1. Heinz-Dieter Hardes, " Prognosemodel der Wohnungsbauinvestitionen", Institut für Siedlung und Wohnunsewesen des Westfälishen Wilhelms-Universität, *Sonderdruck 54,* Münster, 1971. Also see " Enquête über die Bauwirtschaft ", Im Auftrage des Bundesministers für Wirtschaft, 1973.

2. M.J. Hamburger, "Interest Rates and the Demand for Consumer Durable Goods", *American Economic Review,* December 1967.

3. W.H. Branson and A.K. Klevorick, "Money Illusion and the Aggregate Consumption Function", *American Economic Review,* December 1969.

4. F. Modigliani, " Monetary Policy and Consumption – the linkages via interest rate and wealth effects in the FRB-MIT-Penn Model", *Consumer Spending and Monetary Policy,* Federal Reserve Bank of Boston, 1972.

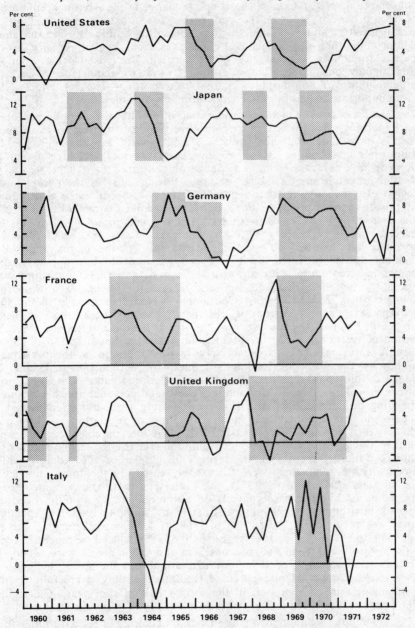

that changes in consumer net worth play the major part among these two channels. In contrast to the findings of single-equation studies, the FMP model also shows an effect of monetary policy on expenditure on consumer non-durables; it suggests that net wealth affects consumption of non-durables

115

as well as durables, while a cost-of-capital effect works only on durables. A partial simulation of the model shows that the percentage decline in total consumption related to a 50 basis-point change in the Treasury bill rate is of the order of 0.13 at the end of the four quarters, and 0.23 by the eighth quarter, and continues to grow thereafter (Table 2). The full simulation finds that the impact is 2-3 times as great as that revealed by the partial simulation. The wealth effect accounts for 70-80 per cent of the total impact on aggregate consumption. Its relative importance reflects the predominance of non-durables in total consumption. The cost effect is the more important of the two effects operating on durables.

In the *United Kingdom,* moderation of private consumption has been an important policy objective in restrictive periods, in order to leave room for the growth of productive investment and exports. For that purpose, the authorities made active use of selective monetary measures such as regulations on hire purchase terms and control on consumer loans (pages 42 and 43) as well as variations on indirect tax rates during most of the period under review. In the first restrictive period (January–October 1960) a slowdown in private consumption set in around the second quarter when hire purchase controls were imposed (Chart 33). The relaxation of controls on hire purchase terms in January 1961 was followed by a sharp rise in consumer spending. It levelled off in the second short period of restraint (July–October 1961) when the banks reduced advances to hire purchase companies in accordance with an official request, and these companies were asked by the authorities not to seek finance for further expansion from sources other than the banks. Consumption recovered quickly in the subsequent expansionary period, at least partly encouraged by the suspension (in April 1962) of the surcharge on customs and excise duties. In the third period of restraint, a rise in the discount rate (the initial action of monetary restraint taken in November 1964) was followed in the subsequent month by the Bank of England's request for a reduction in lending by banks and non-bank financial institutions (including finance houses) for non-priority purposes, notably for hire purchase and personal needs. Consumer spending declined in the first half of the following year, but strengthened in the second half despite the tightening (in June) of regulations on hire purchase terms; it was only from early 1966, when hire purchase controls were further tightened, that private consumption started to decline sharply. It showed a marked recovery in the spring and summer of 1967, during which hire purchase regulations were successively eased. In the fourth restrictive period (late 1967 to early 1971), the initial restrictive package included a tightening of hire purchase controls on automobiles and an official request for all institutions to restrain personal loans, and the consumer spending spree was reversed in the first half of 1968. A further weakening of private consumption occurred in the second half of 1968 when hire purchase regulations were retightened and purchase tax and excise duties were raised. In the easy policy period of 1971 onwards, stimulus in the spring budget and a complete removal of hire purchase regulations in July[1] were followed by a strong rise in consumption in the second half of that year. The regulations were reintroduced in December 1973.

Goodhart's econometric study finds that variables related to hire purchase credit regulations in the current quarter and two quarters earlier are significant in explaining total private consumption. This finding confirms

1. The report by the Crowther Committee on Consumer Credit, published in March 1971, recommended to the Government the abolition of official control over hire purchase terms and extensive changes in the law governing consumer credit.

an earlier study by Ball and Drake[1] and others. Evidence on other channels of monetary policy effects is sparse. Work at Southampton University suggests that capital gains or losses may have a significant effect on spending. But the long-term rate used in Goodhart's equations has no significant role. The treasury also has provisionally drawn negative conclusions about interest rate effects.

In *France*, as in the United Kingdom, the authorities have at times changed regulations on hire purchase terms (see page 41). The pattern of total private consumption was similar in the two restrictive periods (March 1963 to June 1965, and November 1968 to June 1970): it started to decelerate about two quarters after the introduction of restrictive monetary policy and the extent of slowdown (adjusted for the disruptive development in 1968) was also about the same in percentage terms (Chart 33). This similarity seems to reflect the fact that while the growth of personal disposable income was faster in the second phase than in the first period, consumer credit decelerated more sharply as a result of tighter controls on hire purchase terms. The relaxation of hire purchase regulations towards the end of the two restrictive periods was followed by a sharp rise in consumer credit. Another important difference in the monetary developments between these two phases was that interest rates, including deposit rates, were raised sharply on the second occasion. On the other hand, the association between total consumer expenditures and the stance of monetary policy or the development of the financial sector has been at least visually less clear in easy periods. The result of the OECD Secretariat's econometric study suggests, however, that, on average, households' short-term borrowing and the weighted average interest rate on savings and time deposits in the current quarter are useful financial variables in explaining consumption of durables, while only the deposit rate was found useful in the equation for consumption of non-durable manufactured goods.

In *Germany* and *Japan*, private consumption tended to decelerate in restrictive periods and accelerate in easy periods (Chart 33). Cyclical changes in this type of expenditure generally lagged behind investment cycles; the extent of the change (both in percentage and absolute terms) was small relative to those in private inventory and non-residential investment, notably in Japan, but also in Germany. It seems unlikely that changes in monetary policy have a direct impact on private consumption in either country. The wealth effect does not seem significant, given the facts that individual holdings of securities are of little importance and that the variation in wealth resulting from changes in the return on bonds and shares is small relative to the flow of consumption. Consumer credit is gradually developing in both countries, but it still plays only a marginal role as a source of financing. Moreover, no attempt has been made to regulate the terms of consumer credit for demand management purposes.

It is, therefore, not surprising that so far there has been no econometric evidence suggesting direct influence of monetary policy on consumption in these two countries. The Bank of Japan's model[2] separates the equations on private consumption into foodstuffs, durables and others, and even the equation for durables has no financial variables. One of the OECD Secretariat's equations[3] on private consumption in Japan uses as an expla-

1. R.J. Ball and P.S. Drake, "The Impact of Credit Control on Consumer Durable Spending in the United Kingdom, 1957-1961", *the Review of Economic Studies*, Oct. 1963.

2. "The Bank of Japan Econometric Model", Bank of Japan, *Monthly Economic Review*, (in Japanese), Sept. 1972.

3. OECD Monetary Studies Series, *Monetary Policy in Japan*, p. 104.

natory variable the money stock held by the personal sector (adjusted for price changes and lagged two quarters). But given the insignificance of personal borrowing and the small shift from money to other types of financial assets by the personal sector, this variable does not seem to represent the direct effect – the real balance or wealth effect – of monetary policy (see also page 112). In both countries private consumption is considered largely determined by the level of personal disposable income.

However, to the extent that changes in financial conditions affect investment expenditures on these two countries, monetary policy has had an indirect impact on private consumption. In fact, a simulation with the Secretariat's half-yearly model for the Japanese economy (page 102) shows that an increase in the flow of bank credit in the first half year of 1969 (equivalent to a one percentage point increase in its year-to-year growth rate at mid-1969) results in a 0.2 per cent rise in total private consumption in the first half-year and a 0.8 per cent rise in the third half-year, with the impact tapering off subsequently (Table 3). The quantitative illustration of the indirect monetary impact is also possible for Germany, using the Secretariat's quarterly model. A simulation of one half percentage point increase in bond yields from the first quarter of 1969 suggests that the associated decline in private non-food consumption becomes noticeable by the fourth quarter (about 0.2 per cent) and steadily increases thereafter to reach a peak of about 0.6 per cent around the eighth quarter (Table 4). The impact gradually diminishes in the subsequent quarters.

In *Italy*, private consumption has displayed very volatile developments (Chart 33). It started to decelerate before the introduction of restrictive policy in the third quarter of 1963 and fell in 1964 despite the adoption of expansionary policy in the second quarter of that year. The subsequent expansion was reversed in the last quarter of the moderately restrictive period (mid-1969 to third quarter 1970). While this relationship points to the effects of monetary policy on consumption, there have been no firmly established econometric findings linking financial variables directly to private consumption. A recent version of the Bank of Italy's annual model has no financial variables in its equation on consumption; a liquid assets variable used in the earlier versions has been dropped. The quarterly model of the University of Bologna suggests that the increase in liquid assets has a small positive impact, but the long-term bond rate in the current quarter is also used as an explanatory variable with a positive sign. The latter association seems difficult to justify; the sign should be negative if the variable is used to represent either a wealth effect or a cost effect

B. IMPACT ON AGGREGATE DEMAND AND OUTPUT

This section examines the impact of monetary policy on aggregate demand and output. For this purpose, visual observations of aggregate demand and output during various monetary policy phases will be supplemented by a brief survey of available econometric evidence. Broadly, there have been two approaches to the quantitative assessment of the impact of monetary policy actions on aggregate demand and output. The first has been to simulate monetary policy changes using comprehensive econometric models which specify the basic structural relationships of the economic and financial system. The second approach – usually employed in the so-called monetarist contributions – has been to use reduced-form equations which directly associate aggregate demand and output with financial and other variables without specifying the transmission process of monetary policy. In the case of single-equation studies which use intermediate financial variables rather than those under direct control of the monetary authorities, chains of causality are masked, and however good the fit of the equations may be, it is difficult to interpret the impact of monetary policy actions on aggregate demand and output. Despite these shortcomings, such studies will also be reviewed notably for countries where a large-scale model has not yet been constructed or the results of simulations of such models are not yet available.

It is also well known that empirical studies associating nominal aggregate demand alone with short-run changes in relevant monetary variables leave obscure the question as to how much of monetary influences comes in the form of price movement, and how much in output and employment. It makes a vast difference for policy if the primary monetary effect in the short run is on output (and employment) rather than upon prices. In principle, the review of aggregate demand in the following paragraphs will be made in real terms. But for some countries, because of the constraints of econometric evidence, the impact of monetary policy on aggregate demand will be quantitatively assessed only in nominal terms. The impact of monetary policy on prices (GNP deflator) will also be mentioned briefly for countries where econometric findings are available, but no systematic attempt will be made to discuss the experience of the six countries in this respect which has already been summarized in Charts 1 to 6 and the comments thereto.

In the *United States,* the pattern of total demand and output was roughly similar during the two expansionary periods. On the first occasion (1960–1962), a small decline (1.6 per cent) of real GNP in the first year was reversed by a strong rise (average rate of 6.4 per cent) in the following two years; on the second occasion (1967–1971), a slightly smaller fall (1.3 per cent) in the first year was followed by a little less strong rise (4.9 per cent) in the subsequent year. But the development of total demand and output was different between the two periods of restraint. While real GNP maintained high growth (4.9 per cent) in the restrictive period of 1966, it decelerated to a rate (1.2 per cent) well below the past trend during the year 1969. This difference was largely due to a strong rise in public expenditures in the first period; the pattern of total private demand was broadly the same.

There are a number of reduced-form equation studies to assess the effect of monetary (and fiscal) changes on aggregate demand.[1] But their conclusions are unfortunately somewhat divergent. A study by Andersen and Jordan[2] indicates that monetary changes had powerful effects on nominal GNP and that the effects would appear within a year with the long-run multiplier being over 6.50 (Table 5). On the other hand, subsequent investigators critical of the Andersen-Jordan study, who used similar techniques but redefined explanatory monetary (and fiscal) variables, found that the effects of monetary policy can be far smaller. Moreover, it has been shown that the lag differs greatly according to the monetary variable used:[3] it is significantly shorter for money, base money and total reserves (with effects being completed within 4-5 quarters) than for unborrowed

1. See Fisher and Sheppard, *op. cit.*, Part IV.
2. L.C. Andersen and J.L. Jordan, "Monetary and Fiscal Actions: A Test of Their Relative Importance", *Federal Reserve Bank of St. Louis Review*, November 1968.
3. M. Hamburger, "The Lag in the Effect of Monetary Policy", *Federal Reserve Bank of New York Review*, December 1971.

reserves (with less than 40 per cent of the total effect completed within 4-5 quarters).

It is also possible to use large-scale models of the United States economy in assessing the impact of monetary policy changes on aggregate demand.[1] The full simulation with the FMP model suggests that an increase of 50 basis points in the Treasury bill rate reduces real GNF by about half a per cent by the fourth quarter, and 1.4 per cent by the eighth quarter, with no sign of the effect tapering off in the subsequent quarters (Table 2). By the fourth quarter 42 per cent of the reduction in GNP is absorbed by consumption, about 20 per cent by private fixed non-residential investment, 26 per cent by non-farm inventory accumulation, about 17 per cent by residential construction and 10 per cent by state and local government expenditure, while a fall in imports corresponds to about 15 per cent of change in GNP. In the subsequent quarters the contribution of private non-residential investment to the decline in GNP rises, while that of residential construction diminishes. The role of inventory investment in the drop of GNP also becomes less important from around the eighth quarter. The simulation result suggests that there is no noticeable impact on the GNF deflator arising from the assumed change in the Treasury bill rate over the first four quarters, but after eight and twelve quarters there is a slight decline of 0.1 and 0.2 per cent respectively.

In *Japan*, there were clear decelerations of total internal demand and output in periods of monetary restraint (Chart 34). During the first severely restrictive period (July 1961 to October 1962) a sharp deceleration set in around the turn of the year 1961. During the second period of severe monetary restraint (1964) a similarly sharp deceleration started in the second quarter of the year. In the subsequent period of moderate restraint (September 1967 to August 1968) a deceleration of internal demand offset the expansionary impact of the current balance of payments, and the rate of growth of gross national product levelled off in early 1968. In the last period of mild restraint (September 1969 to October 1970) economic deceleration set in around mid-1970. The pattern of aggregate demand in easy periods was somewhat less regular. While the acceleration of total demand in the easy period of 1963 was prompt and sharp, a strong recovery in the subsequent period of expansionary policy (early 1965 to September 1967) started in early 1966, with a delay of about a year. In the neutral policy period of autumn 1968 to late 1969, maintenance of rapid growth without further acceleration was consistent with the stance of policy. During the period from late 1970 onwards when active expansionary monetary policy was adopted, a sharp rise in demand and output started in early 1972,

It is possible to use the OECD Secretariat's half-yearly model in assessing the impact of monetary policy on aggregate demand, since bank credit expansion (an exogenous variable in the model) may be viewed as subject to the control of the monetary authorities. A simulation was run in which it was assumed that bank credit expansion increased in the first half-year of 1969 to such an extent as to raise the year-to-year growth rate at mid-1969 by one percentage point, returning to the actually observed path thereafter. This exercise shows that the associated percentage rise in real GNP increases from about 0.7 in the first half-year to a range of between 1.2 and 1.4 in the subsequent two half-years and diminishes to about 0.5 in the fourth half-year (Table 3). The distribution of the impact on aggregate demand among major demand components is also an impor-

---

1. Fisher and Sheppard, *op. cit.*, Part III.

Chart 34. TOTAL INTERNAL DEMAND AND OUTPUT

Constant prices, seasonally adjusted annual rate of change over previous quarter, three quarter moving average

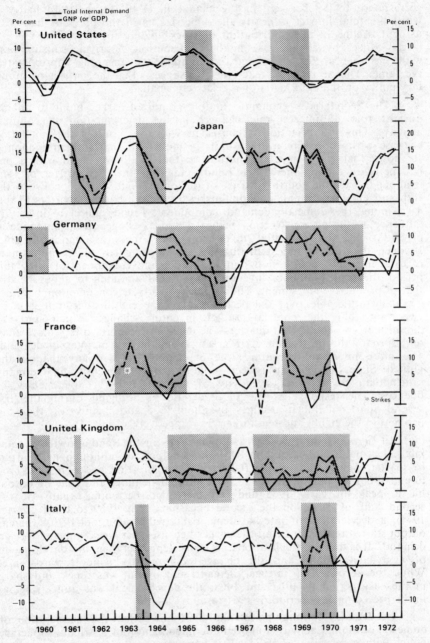

tant concern of the monetary authorities. The Secretariat's study finds that in the second half-year, roughly 60 per cent of the total increase in real GNF shows up in private non-residential fixed investment, about 30 per

121

cent in private stockbuilding, about a quarter in private consumption and 2-3 per cent in private residential investment. The rise in imports amounts to about 15 per cent of the change in GNP, while the decline in exports corresponds to 2-3 per cent of the change in GNP. In the third half-year when the total impact is nearly the same size as in the previous half-year, a slight decline in the contribution of stockbuilding to the rise in GNF is largely offset by an increase in the contribution of private consumption, with the role of the other demand components remaining approximately the same. The Secretariat's exercise also suggests that the impact of monetary policy on the GNP deflator is relatively small.

The Secretariat's economic findings reported earlier point to an important role of interest rate changes in the determination of economic activity. This interpretation is consistent with the result of the simulation exercise with the Secretariat's quarterly model for the German economy. It shows that the percentage decline in real GNP associated with a one half percentage point increase in bond yields from the first quarter of 1969 is about 0.4 by the fourth quarter, of the order of 0.5 to 0.6 between the fifth and eighth quarters, and diminishes in the subsequent quarters (Table 4). Among the domestic demand components found subject to monetary influence — housing construction being treated as exogenous in the model — private fixed non-residential investment plays the most important role. Between the fourth and sixth quarters, more than half of the adjustment of total internal demand shows up in this demand component. During this period the contribution of inventory investment amounts to about half of that of productive investment. The response of private consumption becomes gradually noticeable over the period and by the eighth quarter it is more important than the contribution of inventory changes which starts to diminish from around that quarter. The decline in imports offset more than one third of the impact on GNF arising from the fall in internal demand. The more important offsetting role of imports in Germany than in the United States and Japan reflects higher import propensity in Germany rather than the stronger sensitivity of German imports to monetary influences. The response of the GNP deflator is negligible during the first several quarters. But it declines by about 0.25 and slightly less than 0.4 per cent in the eighth and tenth quarters respectively (Table 4).

In *Germany,* there were clear downswings in the trend growth of total internal demand and output in two restrictive periods, although its quarter-to-quarter change was volatile (Chart 34). On the first occasion (mid-1964 to end-1966) the rate of growth of total internal demand and that of output hit a peak in early 1965 and fell thereafter, becoming negative in the second half of 1966; on the second occasion (early 1969 to third quarter 1971), a deceleration of internal demand started around mid-1970, whereas output started to decelerate a little earlier because of a weakening of foreign demand. It is more difficult to observe consistency between the development of aggregate demand and the change of monetary policy towards ease. While the recovery of internal demand and output was quick and sharp in the easy period of 1967 and 1968, the development was quite irregular in the preceding easy period of 1961 to mid-1964.

In *France,* turning point analysis shows that the deceleration of domestic economic activity followed the introduction of restrictive monetary policy with a relatively short delay (Chart 34). On the first occasion (1963 to mid-1965), the growth of GDP started to slow down around mid-1964; on the second occasion (late 1968 to mid-1970) a moderate deceleration in economic activity set in towards the end of 1969. In easy periods, except for the years 1967-68, a quick and strong upswing of economic activity was not observed: instead, rather smooth growth was maintained.

The Bank of France's simplified quarterly model of the French economy provides information on the quantitative assessment of monetary influences on aggregate demand.[1] In one of its equations, the change in the value of industrial production is explained by variables including *i*) changes in the broadly defined money supply in the current and the preceding five quarters; *ii*) changes in an indicator of fiscal policy in the current and the preceding five quarters; and *iii*) changes in exports in the current and the preceding three quarters. The equation for changes in the money supply uses, as an explanatory variable, changes in the rate of interest on bank advances in the current quarter and a quarter earlier. Non-monetary explanatory variables used are price changes and wage changes (in the current quarter and a quarter earlier) as well as an indicator of employment, which are in turn explained by other equations. The model suggests that a one per cent increase in the money supply is associated with a 0.6 per cent rise in industrial production in value terms, spread over the current and the following five quarters (Chart 35); and that a one percentage point decline in the interest rate is related to a one per cent rise in output over the same period.

In the *United Kingdom*, it is difficult to generalize the pattern of internal demand and output in periods of monetary restraint and ease on the basis of turning point analysis (Chart 34). The deceleration of internal demand and output started immediately after the introduction of restrictive policy in early 1960. Output rose in the subsequent period of monetary ease, largely reflecting a rise in foreign demand, while internal demand remained sluggish. Both internal demand and output weakened in the second, short-lived, period of restraint. Aggregate domestic demand and output strengthened from the year 1964, but tended to slow down in the restrictive period of 1965-66. During the subsequent periods of monetary ease and restraint, total internal demand displayed large swings in directions consistent with the stance of policy, but the fluctuations in output were much smaller. In fact the rise in domestic demand in the easy period of 1967 was largely met by the growth of imports, and output activity stagnated. On the other hand, the impact on output of the slowdown in internal demand in the following restrictive period was at least partly offset by the gradual strengthening of the foreign balance helped by the devaluation of sterling in late 1967. A rise in total internal demand and output in the last reflationary period occurred somewhat faster than in the similar phase of 1962-64. This was due largely to a quicker recovery in private consumption, which reflected stimulus in the budget of spring 1971 and subsequent fiscal measures and the removal of hire purchase regulations.

No large-scale model is available in the United Kingdom to quantify monetary impacts on aggregate demand and output. Artis and Nobay[2] constructed a number of reduced-form equations directly linking nominal GDP with monetary variables as well as indicators of fiscal policy. They tested, as appropriate monetary indicators, two measures of the money supply, bank advances and two measures of the monetary base, and found the broad money supply as the most promising among them. This monetary indicator was found to affect nominal GDP with a lag varying from

1. J.H. David, "Un modèle de l'économie française inspiré des thèses monétaristes", Banque de France, *Bulletin Trimestriel*, November 1972.
2. M.J. Artis and A.R. Nobay, "Two Aspects of the Monetary Debate", *National Institute Economic Review*, August 1969.

Chart 35. LAG PATTERNS OF MONETARY AND FISCAL IMPACTS ON INDUSTRIAL OUTPUT: FRANCE

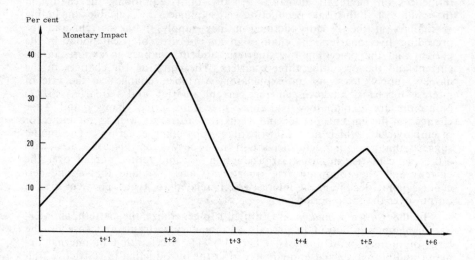

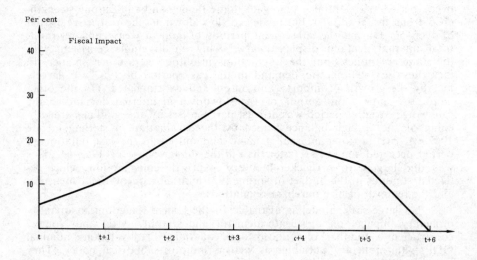

Note : The size of the impact in the quarter (t + i) arising from a change in the monetary (fiscal) indicator in the quarter t is shown as per cent of the total impact.

Source : J.H. David, « Un modèle de l'économie française inspiré des thèses monétaristes », Banque de France, *Bulletin Trimestriel*, November 1972.

124

two to four quarters according to equations (Table 5). The lag was considerably longer than that for fiscal indicators. Moreover, the money multiplier was far smaller (0.1 − 0.2 by the end of six quarters) than the fiscal multiplier (3.3 − 6.6 by that time).[1] However, the fit of most of the equations was poor and the authors thought that not too much reliance should be placed on the results of their work.

Research at the Bank of England[2] has tested the strength and predictability of the relationship between the money stock (M1, M2 and M3) and income levels (GDP and industrial output in money terms), using first differences of the data and with and without a constant term in the equations. The fit of the equations was better when industrial output, instead of GDP, was used as the dependent variable. This finding implies that the money stock has a closer relationship with industrial production than output in other sectors of the economy. Among the three measures of money, M3 performed best. Where the constant term was suppressed, the explanatory power of the monetary variable increased. The changes in M3 in the current quarter and in the immediately preceding quarters were of some significance, although those in two and four quarters earlier have more important explanatory power. In general, the lag was shorter and the long-run money multiplier was larger (0.3 − 0.9) than suggested by the Artis-Nobay study.

In *Italy*, there were two phases of slowdown in domestic demand and output during the period under review (Chart 34). The first one started around September 1963 (when disinflationary monetary policy was introduced) and was preceded by a sharp downturn in monetary aggregates which set in around the end of 1962. The second downturn in total domestic demand started in early 1970, about two quarters after the introduction of restrictive policy. Output had already begun to decelerate towards the end of 1968, but this was largely due to persistent social unrest and political instability, i.e. factors other than those which are related to short-run demand management policy.

Quantitative estimates of financial influences on aggregate demand based on the simulation of large-scale models are unfortunately not available for Italy. But there are some simple studies which tested the relationship between economic activity and monetary changes. In Keran's equation,[3] changes in economic activity (measured by the proxy variable based on industrial production index and consumer price index) were explained by changes in the money stock lagged three quarters. The estimated value of the money multiplier was slightly below 2, but the fit of the equation was poor. In fact, since the cyclical instability of the Italian economy has not been pronounced during most of the period examined (1953–1968) except for the sharp fall in 1963, the conclusions of the study have been dominated by the relationship between the development of output and that of the monetary variable in 1962–63. And, if the fact is taken into account that the slowdown in monetary expansion in 1963 started well before the introduction of restrictive policy, it may be difficult to establish a causal relationship running from monetary policy changes to economic activity

1. This result is in contrast with the study by Andersen and Jordan quoted above according to which the money and fiscal multipliers for the United States are 6.6 and 0.2 respectively by the end of the 6th quarter (Table 5).
2. "The Importance of Money", Appendix II; "Money Multiplier", *Bank of England Quarterly Bulletin*, June 1970.
3. M.E. Keran, "Monetary and Fiscal Influences on Economic Activity: The Foreign Experience", *Federal Reserve Bank of St. Louis Review*, February 1970.

solely on the basis of this study. Sitzia tested the relative importance of monetary and fiscal influences on economic activity also through a single equation approach for the period from the first quarter 1955 to third quarter 1969.[1] His equation associating economic activity with monetary influences (both measured by the same indicators used by Keran) suggested a long-run money multiplier (after 6 quarters) of about 2.7. The multiplier was reduced when he introduced a fiscal indicator measured by total cash outlays of the central government (Table 5). The equation became very unstable when exports were added as a third explanatory variable. It remained so, even when different sample periods were used, and the author concluded that not too much confidence should be placed on the result of single-equation studies without structural estimation.

1. Bruno Sitzia, "Monetary and Fiscal Influences on Economic Activity: the Italian Experience", *unpublished* paper, M.I.T., September 1971.

Table 4. GERMANY: RESPONSE OF REAL EXPENDITURES TO AN INCREASE IN BOND YIELDS OF 1/2 PERCENTAGE POINT AT END OF 1968

	1969 Q2		1969 Q4		1970 Q2		1970 Q4		1971 Q2	
	% Dev.[1]	% of GNP[2]	% Dev.	% of GNP	% Dev.	% of GNP	% Dev.	% of GNP	% Dev.	% of GNP
Private non-residential fixed investment	−0.06	−0.01	−2.03	−0.34	−2.68	−0.46	−2.75	−0.48	−2.55	−0.46
Inventory investment	−3.72	−0.09	−5.45	−0.15	−8.46	−0.22	−6.03	−0.18	−0.67	−0.02
Private consumption (non food)	−0.03	−0.01	−0.21	−0.08	−0.45	−0.18	−0.62	−0.24	−0.58	−0.23
Imports	−0.19	+0.04	−0.75	+0.18	−1.21	+0.30	−1.38	+0.37	−1.23	+0.34
GNP	−0.07	−0.07	−0.39	−0.39	−0.56	−0.56	−0.54	−0.54	−0.38	−0.38
GNP deflator	−0.01	−	−0.03	−	−0.12	−	−0.26	−	−0.36	−

1. Percentage deviation of the value of the expenditure variable calculated on the basis of the assumed level of bond yields (i.e. 1/2 percentage point higher than observed) from the value of that variable in the corresponding quarter determined by the model using the actual level of bond yields.

2. Contribution to the percentage change in GNP.
Source: Simulation with the OECD Secretariat's quarterly model of the German economy.

Table 5. MONETARY AND FISCAL MULTIPLIERS

Estimates by Almon lag technique

	United States (Andersen-Jordan)		United Kingdom (Artis-Nobay)				Italy (Sitzia)			
			Equation A		Equ. B	Equ. C	Equ. A	Equ. B	Equation C	
	ΔMS	ΔT	ΔMS	ΔGFM	ΔMS	ΔGFM	ΔMS	ΔGE	ΔMS	ΔGE
After 1 quarter	1.6	0.2	nil	1.9	nil	2.7	0.5	0.1	0.3	0.1
After 2 quarters	3.5	0.2	nil	3.4	nil	3.8	1.2	0.4	0.9	0.3
After 3 quarters	5.3	0.2	nil	3.8	0.1	3.0	1.9	0.9	1.5	0.6
After 4 quarters	6.6	0.2	0.1	3.3	0.2	2.3	2.5	1.4	1.9	0.9
After 5 quarters	6.6	0.2	0.1	3.3	0.2	3.6	2.7	1.8	2.1	1.2
After 6 quarters	6.6	0.2	0.1	3.3	0.2	6.6	2.7	2.1	2.0	1.4

Key :   MS = money supply
   T = taxes
GFM = government fiscal measures
GE = cash outlay by the central government
Δ = quarterly changes.

130

V

CONCLUDING REMARKS

The purpose of the present study has been to survey, on a comparative basis, the experience of six countries — France, Germany, Italy, Japan, the United Kingdom and the United States — in the use of monetary policy for shorter-run demand management purposes. By drawing together the main results of the surveys of countries individually, published in the *OECD Monetary Studies Series,* and additional evidence which has become available since these surveys were completed, it is hoped to bring out some general conclusions on the working of monetary policy. More specifically, the study is intended to be of assistance to officials in central banks, Treasuries and other agencies engaged in the valuation of the internal and external effects of monetary phenomena in other countries. The understanding of monetary phenomena in other countries is often hampered by differences in terminology, by institutional peculiarities or simply by the lack of material in comparable form.

An undertaking of this type is unfortunately subject to rapid obsolescence. One major limitation is that the terminal point for most of the surveys of individual countries on which the present study is based was at the end of 1971. While subsequent developments in the use of instruments have been included, the systematic evaluation of policy effects does not include most of the experiences gained over the last three years, and particularly the use of monetary policy to cool off the unprecedented parallel boom in the OECD area in 1972-73. There are, for this reason also, only few references to the implications for monetary policy of the greater flexibility of exchange rates since the summer of 1971. Though the freedom of action gained has not been as great as initially perceived, this omission is serious to someone primarily interested in the current applicability of the main results.

A further limitation of the study from such a perspective is that the period 1960-1971 (or 72) to which the analysis applies was rather different in policy orientation from recent concerns. Though there was some acceleration of prices towards the end of the period, it would not be much of an exaggeration to say that the main internal task of monetary policy was seen as one of stabilizing real demand at a level commensurate with current productive capacity. The longer-run linkages from monetary variables to price developments and the role of monetary policy in dampening cost inflation were not nearly as much in the forefront of policy debates as they have been recently. This is why the present study focuses on the impact on the major components of real demand and on the current and

131

the capital account of the balance of payments, though some evidence is presented also on the impact of the rate of change of the GNF deflator and other price series.

With these limitations in mind, the main questions may be posed as follows:

i) How important were the total effects on real demand of monetary actions taken?

ii) To what transmission channels may they be attributed?

iii) Did their timing pattern create problems, long lags contributing to destabilization rather than the opposite?

iv) Was the sectoral impact broadly acceptable?

v) How did the current account respond to monetary restraint and ease?

vi) How were private capital flows and international reserves influenced?

vii) How close was the control over major domestic financial variables?

viii) What are the implications of these findings for the design of monetary policy and use of instruments?

Only partial and preliminary answers can, of course, be given to most of these far-ranging questions; nevertheless, the attempt must be made. In making it, the order of summarizing the conclusions will be the reverse of that followed in the main body of the report which proceeded from a discussion of instruments via their impact in domestic financial markets and on external capital flows to their impact on major components of real demand. Having some information on the latter impact should, however, be helpful in reviewing some of the other issues.

The total impact of monetary policy is considerable in all six countries. The evidence is clearest for the United States and Japan, which is particularly interesting since these two countries represent opposites among the countries surveyed with respect to their use of monetary instruments. In the United States, simulations with large-scale econometric models suggest that a sustained increase in short-term money market rates (represented by the Treasury bill rate) of $\frac{1}{2}$ percentage point has tended to cut real GNP by one-half per cent after four quarters and twice that after six quarters. The increase in short-term rates during restrictive phases beyond what would have occurred as a result of demand factors can only be determined in a very approximate way; but it is a fact that bill rates have gone up substantially more than $\frac{1}{2}$ percentage point during restrictive phases. In the course of the 1969 restriction the bill rate rose by around 2 percentage points, a development which may have reduced real GNP by as much as $1\frac{1}{2}$ per cent by mid-1970. This is clearly a substantial effect in the light of average annual increases in GNP of 4-5 per cent. In Japan, a one percentage point modification of the growth rate of bank credit – approximately policy controlled – appears to have entailed a change in the same direction of the growth rate of real GNP by two-thirds of a percentage point within six months and about twice that after a full year. Policy-induced changes in bank credit growth rates have typically been of the order of 5 per cent, suggesting that monetary restraint during the active phases of the 1960s may have cut as much as 5-6 per cent of real GNP about a year after the onset of restraint. This is close to half the annual rate of growth of Japanese real GNP in the 1960-1970 period – again a very substantial effect. Though the precise magnitude of these effects is subject to considerable uncertainty, their order is impressive.

132

The evidence from other countries does not suggest effects quite that important. Nevertheless, variations in German bond rates appear to have been significant, a one percentage point increase being associated with a decline in real GNP at the end of four quarters of somewhat less than one half per cent. The impact of monetary policy appears to have been weaker in France, Italy and the United Kingdom than in the other three countries, though some of the explanation in the case of France may lie in the fact that the countercyclical element in French policy has not been very strong. There is in all three countries evidence of both rationing effects and responses to interest rate changes. While the evidence from France, Italy and the United Kingdom is preliminary, more informal inspection of developments in phases of active policy as well as the views of policy-makers suggests that an active monetary policy can contribute in important ways to demand management also in these three countries. The magnitude of the policy effects may not approach those of major fiscal changes of the type introduced e.g. in the United Kingdom since 1967; but they are neither so weak in total, nor so slow in coming, that they can not contribute in a major way to demand management from year to year.

There are clear differences in the relative importance of the various *transmission channels* among the six countries. In the United States, the major effects come through changes in interest rates; they influence non-residential fixed investment by modifying the cost of capital and private consumption by a combined cost and wealth effect. Though the wealth effect has possibly been somewhat overstated in recent research, it is an important feature of the transmission process in the United States that the market value of household financial wealth changes under the impact of monetary policy. Rationing or availability effects have been conclusively identified only in the mortgage market; with this one important exception — accounting for 10-15 per cent of the impact on real GNP — the U.S. financial system must be viewed as one in which markets tend to be cleared within relatively short periods of time by movements in interest rates and where particular observed flows of credit generally can not be interpreted to have had causal significance.

Japan offers the main contrast to the U.S. experiences. Not only has the main burden of restraint typically fallen relatively harder on business investment and much less on private consumption and residential construction, but rationing effects have been clearly identifiable. The heavy reliance by Japanese enterprises on external funds, mainly bank borrowing, and the difficulty of substituting the latter by other sources have assured that any important deceleration of bank lending would lead to a quick and sizeable slowdown in corporate investment. This has been the dominant modus operandi of Japanese monetary policy; interest rates have moved comparatively little, and the size of any indirect effects on consumption and residential construction has been modest.

The other four countries are intermediate cases though the empirical work surveyed suggests that they are rather closer to the U.S. model than generally recognized. While rationing elements have by no means been absent, it is interesting to note that they do not dominate in France and Italy where, for reasons of public interventions or institutional rigidities, they must a priori be assumed important; in both countries links from interest rate changes to private fixed investment have been found. In the United Kingdom, availability effects are important in the mortgage market where rates move sluggishly. While they were also important in restraining

133

household durable consumption prior to 1971, it is noteworthy that the credit ceilings then practised did not have any detectable impact on private fixed investment, reflecting the highly developed state of the markets for longer-term finance. Finally, in Germany the impact of monetary policy on fixed and inventory investment has been transmitted primarily through interest rate changes. Only in the United Kingdom, among the four intermediate countries, does the household sector hold an important portfolio of fixed interest securities or shares, the market value of which would change as interest rates move; more generally the data necessary for testing the strength of a wealth effect through fluctuations in the value of household financial and physical assets are not available for the countries.

While the total effects of monetary policy must be considered to be substantial over the time horizon typically relevant to policy makers, i.e. six to twelve months, *the tendency for effects to continue to build up over time* does present serious problems of potential instability. To achieve desired significant effects within a year, fairly large changes in instruments may have to be envisaged, provided of course that they are financially feasible; but the effects of such changes are likely to cumulate beyond the present policy horizon to cyclically inappropriate proportions. The protracted responses of an economy and the phenomenon of " over-shooting " associated with an active countercyclical policy require corrective action to be taken at a later date; the stronger these characteristics, the more policy instruments may have to move over time, generating financial instability to an undesired extent. These arguments justify, in the eyes of some observers, greater reliance on monetary rules, particularly stable growth rates of the major monetary aggregates over longer periods, in preference to actively countercyclical policies. This is an issue which can not be resolved in general terms; that would involve both a deeper analysis of the time pattern of responses to monetary changes and a judgement on the relative size of monetary and non-monetary disturbances in the various economies. The most that can be safely concluded is that the potential contribution of monetary policy to demand management over a six to twelve month horizon has been so considerable as to make it unlikely that the disadvantages of longer-term instability could outweigh it.

The *sectoral impact of monetary policy* has been highly uneven. In Japan and Germany, private non-residential fixed investment and inventory accumulation have accounted for the major part of the adjustment to changes in the monetary stance. In the other economies private investment has also tended to be more volatile than other components of domestic demand, but the generally much lower investment propensity has constrained the monetary authorities in the extent to which they have been prepared to restrain investment and thus slow down the growth of productive capacity. The authorities have aimed at directing a larger part of the impact towards private consumption, particularly of durables. The effects on housebuilding have also been important; indeed they have at times been considered unacceptably severe, and the authorities in the United Kingdom and the United States have on occasions found it necessary to act to assure this sector of a larger inflow of funds than the rigidities of the mortgage markets permitted. These examples underline that an uneven sectoral impact may often constrain the vigour with which changes in monetary policy can be introduced.

To the extent that monetary policy has been effective in influencing private expenditures, there has been an *impact on the current account,* particularly through the import side, the magnitude depending mainly on the marginal import propensity which varies from a low of less than 10 per cent for the United States to nearly three times that in the European economies surveyed. Besides, exports, have been shown to respond to changes in domestic demand pressures in some economies, notably Germany, Japan and Italy. When monetary restraint was applied to halt a deterioration in the current account it was most often successful; particularly clear examples may be found in Japan and Italy during the 1960s. In other cases such an effect came about as a by-product of domestically-motivated restraint. Since dilemma situations in which the external and internal policy aims were in conflict appear to have been rare, the record of monetary policy in the adjustment of the current account points to a useful role. An important exception was the United States, where the current account showed limited cyclical sensitivity around a deteriorating trend.

The degree of financial openness of the six economies and accordingly *the sensitivity of the capital account to changes in relative monetary conditions* varies greatly between the six countries. It has been the smallest in Japan which has had the tightest system of controls of private capital flows. It has not been very much greater in France. While the problem of capital flows offsetting policy-induced changes in domestic monetary conditions has been effectively limited in these two countries, the disturbances from speculative capital flows have been violent at times. In the other four countries, the size of capital flows induced by changes in the relative stance of domestic monetary policy has been larger. The authorities have in a number of cases relied on such relationships to protect the level of their international reserves — the United Kingdom prior to the 1967 devaluation of sterling and Italy in 1969 being the typical examples. At other times policy-induced capital flows have made the domestic tasks of the monetary authorities harder without any compensating external benefits. The leading examples are Germany's attempts to cool off the booms of 1960–61 and 1969–1970 by tighter monetary policies; a very large part of the policy effects were offset through capital inflows leading to an undesired swelling of Germany's international reserves. These experiences led the German authorities to use additional instruments of capital control, notably on the inflows of non-bank funds; and they increased Germany's acceptance of upward floating. It is interesting to note, however, that except for short periods in 1970 when speculative pressures were intense, some degree of monetary autonomy was preserved even in the German case; the external offset was less complete.

The experiences of the United States are in a special category. There is evidence of significant responsiveness of short-term flows to domestic policy actions, though the degree of offset was much smaller than in, say, Germany or Italy. But the impact on domestic monetary conditions was relatively weak. This was because the external imbalances generated were reflected largely in shifts of U.S. short-term liabilities between foreign official institutions and other holders. Moreover, given the size of domestic financial markets, any domestic monetary effect arising from very large external deficits could have been offset by open market operations. While U.S. monetary policy for these reasons preserved a particularly high degree of autonomy, the design of policy was at times influenced by external considerations. These actions — the main one known as Operation Twist in 1961–64 — met with limited success, because it proved difficult to modify the term structure of interest rates in the required way.

The degree of control over domestic financial variables in any one country is to a large extent determined by the magnitude and predictability of the external financial linkages. The larger and the more unpredictable the impact of instrument changes on external capital flows, the more tenuous is the degree of control over domestic monetary aggregates. When, furthermore, the main domestic source of increases in the money supply — the expansion of bank credit — is subject to administrative control as has been the case in Japan and France, the generally higher degree of control over the monetary aggregates and the relative smoothness of their growth rates are not surprising. The response of these variables to monetary actions elsewhere has been slower and at times erratic, notably in Germany and the United Kingdom. The United States represents an intermediate case; within shorter periods of three to six months growth rates of the aggregates have not reflected policy actions at all closely, whereas average growth rates over longer periods of a year or so appear to have corresponded rather well with intentions at the time. There is, however, little doubt that quarterly growth rates of the aggregates could be made to conform fairly closely to a wide range of chosen targets if the authorities were determined to achieve this. Considerations of the evidence on the real impact of monetary policy suggest that insistence on precise, short-term targets is not necessary for stabilizing purposes. Although an apparent greater looseness in the money supply function should not be overemphasized, the linkages have seemed so weak in some policy phases in Germany, Italy and the United Kingdom, that the intentions of policy have been unable to make themselves felt.

The impact on long-term interest rates is a crucial factor in the evaluation of policy effectiveness in view of their important role in the transmission process. This impact is not necessarily the clearest in countries where the authorities intervene directly or administratively in long-term markets (as has been the case in Italy or France for example) because such interventions typically contain a large element of either structural considerations or of accommodation, which at times limits the use of open market operations for countercyclical policies. The impact is also clear when it is more indirect as in Germany or the United States. In financial markets where long-term rates seem to be primarily explained by present and expected short rates, the time lags involved in achieving desired effects appear to be rather longer than comfortable. A further difficulty in assuming that the thrust from changes in long-term rates is cyclically appropriate is the apparent sluggishness of these rates in reflecting shifts in inflationary expectations. Quantification of such shifts is hazardous, but within a wide range of possible measures it would appear that real long-term rates have moved pro-cyclically in several phases of active policy in recent years. The longer-term trend of real rates has been downward as inflationary expectations have become stronger; and the monetary authorities have reinforced this trend by their reluctance to accept higher nominal rates. This factor is undoubtedly underestimated in the many references to extreme tightness in official evaluations of restrictive policies during the 1972–73 boom.

The range of policy instruments used has tended to widen over time. In the process the important differences between countries have narrowed. Financial markets have widened considerably in countries where they were relatively weak in the early postward period — Germany and Japan are the main examples — thereby increasing the scope and efficiency of securities operations. The discount mechanism has come to be used more flexibly, notably by frequent changes in the discount rate (Italy, United States) or by linking it to market rates (United Kingdom). While these tendencies and the diminishing use of outright administrative intervention in interest rate formation have increased the price-oriented element in the functioning of monetary policy, there are also opposite tendencies to be observed. The use of credit ceilings has been spreading after a period of apparent disfavour, and regulations of external capital flows have been considerably reinforced, though hardly in step with the increase in amplitude of such flows. But, on balance, there can be little doubt that the development has been towards greater reliance on the price mechanism in financial markets. Interest rates have been permitted to move over wider ranges in the course of the period under study; the political and technical constraints appear to have weakened. Only the United Kingdom has labelled this evolution a reform of monetary policy, and it may have come about more abruptly there than elsewhere.

In permitting and encouraging developments in this direction, the monetary authorities have been guided by an expectation of gains in efficiency of financial markets in allocating credit and by the greater capacity of these markets to sustain large shifts in fund flows without requiring crisis interventions. But it has also been an important consideration that monetary policy relying on interest rate effects can also influence economic activity efficiently as is demonstrated by the substantial impact of monetary policy in the United States and Germany. The implication of a competitive financial system for the design of monetary policy is that precise targets for particular financial flows are not particularly useful; interest rates can often be more appropriate targets. However, changing inflationary expectations make it hazardous to use observed nominal interest rates as an indicator of the thrust of monetary policy; on the other hand, real interest rates cannot be simply observed from available data. In this context, it has been argued that the money stock can generally provide a better indicator of policy thrust, notably in periods of changing price expectations. But the review of the experiences, particularly in countries with a flexible financial system, suggests that various measures of the money stock often show divergent movements. Rigid adherence to a particular definition of a monetary aggregate would have led to mismanagement of most economies in some policy phases. There is no substitute for continuous re-examination of the stability of the various relationships that enter into the transmission process.

Many efforts have in recent years gone into the empirical work necessary for such a re-examination, particularly in the United States. The main consideration in choosing an operating target optimal from the viewpoint of stabilizing demand is the relative degree of predictability in the private expenditure, money demand and money supply functions. If expenditures are particularly volatile, a target for reserve money (monetary base) or possibly bank credit is likely to be the most reliable. If unpredictability is an important feature of the demand of private non-banks for financial assets, a target for interest rates is likely to be superior. Evidence on the past stability of these relationships is, therefore, relevant to the selection of an optimal target. But past behaviour is not necessarily a good guide to the present choice, as the authorities of most countries have learned in recent years from the experiences with financial innovations, shifts in banks' and non-banks' behaviour generated by uncertainty, and sharp external disturbances. The downward shift of the demand for free liquid assets by German banks and the upward shift of the non-banks' demand for most definitions of the monetary aggregates in selected recent phases in the United Kingdom and the United States are important examples of the dangers inherent in any mechanical extrapolations of past experiences in the monetary field. Such situations do not justify a casual attitude towards the choice of targets; on the contrary, they point to the need for intensified efforts of analysis into financial behaviour and its interrelationship with developments in the markets for goods and services. The many studies done at (or sponsored by) the central banks of the six countries here surveyed testify that a need for widening the analytical basis for monetary policy is felt also among those responsible for designing and implementing policy.

A NOTE ON CRITERIA FOR SELECTING
AN OPTIMAL TARGET FOR MONETARY POLICY

The development of procedures for selecting an optimal target for monetary policy has been clarified in recent years in a number of important contributions by economists of the Federal Reserve System.[1] The following presentation builds mainly on a survey by Victor Argy.[2]

As in any theoretical argument, analysis of the choice of an optimal target proceeds from assumptions which may seem restrictive in the light of the variety of practical problems encountered in monetary management. In the following it will be assumed that there is only one ultimate policy objective – a decision level of income (or employment). The monetary authorities are assumed to have a choice among a number of financial targets: a short-term interest rate, the monetary base, total bank reserves, unborrowed reserves, the bank liquidity ratio and domestic credit expansion. These targets correspond to a number of the financial targets surveyed for the six countries; but it is now assumed that each target, if chosen, is completely controllable within the horizon relevant for policy through available policy instruments, though this is not, in the light of the discussion above, a realistic assumption with respect to several of the targets. Then the crucial point in monetary management is the choice of the target which maximizes the precision with which one may expect to achieve the ultimate objective.

If all relationships in the economy were known with certainty, the choice would be trivial: each of the six financial targets would, in principle, provide an accurate guide to attaining the ultimate objective. In reality, all economic relationships are subject to a greater or smaller element of uncertainty. To choose the optimal target one needs to specify the nature of these uncertainties. It may, in turn, be assumed that the policy makers

1. For a review of the U.S. discussion, see OECD Monetary Studies Series, *Monetary Policy in the United States*, Appendix II. The main contributions have been W. Poole, "Rules of Thumb for Guiding Monetary Policy", in *Open Market Policies and Operating Procedures*, Federal Reserve Board 1971, and J. Pierce and T. Thomson, "Controlling the Money Stock", in *Controlling the Monetary Aggregates II: The Implementation*, Federal Reserve Bank of Boston 1972. Victor Argy has generalized the theory; see below. A further important contribution is B. Friedman, "Targets. Instruments and Indicators of Monetary Policy", *Harvard Institute of Economic Research Discussion Paper 347*, February 1974.

2. This note draws on work carried out by Victor Argy when he was a consultant to the OECD. His work is reported in "An Evaluation of Financial Targets in Six Countries", *Banca Nazionale del Lavoro Quarterly Review*, March 1974, in which references to the voluminous literature may also be found.

have made errors in their assessment of five economic variables: private expenditures, the demand for money, the demand for currency, the demand for reserve money from the banks and the change in net foreign assets of the consolidated banking system (i.e. the balance on official settlements). It is then possible by means of a simple Keynesian economic model[1] to study to what extent the choice of the various financial targets affects the accuracy with which the income aim is achieved, as each of these errors is considered in turn.

If the authorities make an erroneous forecast, say an underestimate, of *private expenditures,* a policy designed to achieve a monetary base target would achieve maximum stabilization. The non-bank public would in this situation want to hold a larger volume of both bank deposits and currency than anticipated, thereby diminishing the reserves available to banks while increasing the need for reserves. Banks will restrain credit, and interest rates will tend to rise, thereby constraining the deviation of expenditures from the forecast level. Such an effect would be somewhat less important if policy was formulated in terms of total reserves; the banks would accommodate some of the increased demand for money by reducing excess reserves which are sensitive to interest rate changes. The maintenance of unborrowed reserves at a targeted level would be even more destabilizing, because the banks would then offset the unexpected drain in bank reserves through additional borrowing facilities at the central bank. The elements of accommodation would be complete and stabilization of private expenditures accordingly absent in the case of an interest rate target or a liquidity ratio target. It is more difficult to rank a policy aiming at a domestic credit expansion target; it will be stabilizing to the extent that the net effect of the upwards shift in expenditures is to reduce the country's international reserves and thereby the money supply below what they would otherwise have been. Whether this happens depends on the relative size of the worsening of the current account and the capital inflow induced by the tendency for domestic interest rates to rise. Only if the former dominates, as it will typically do in countries which are not closely integrated financially with other economies (Japan in the 1960s may be the leading example), will a DCE target be stabilizing in the face of a shift in private expenditures. In countries where the response of the capital account to fluctuations in domestic activity is pronounced (Germany until recently), a DCE target is more likely to be destabilizing.

The conclusions are quite different when the disturbance arises in the financial sector. One might envisage an upward *shift in the non-bank sector's demand for bank deposits* (and thereby money) *or a shift in the components of money holdings* (deposits and currency). Private expenditures are assumed to be on their forecast course and the optimal policy is one that will to a maximum extent offset the financial shifts, thus insulating the goods market from any undesired impact. The targets best equipped to secure this objective are interest rates and the bank liquidity ratio; if they are watched, additional reserves will be supplied to accommodate the needs of banks. There would also be some tendency towards accommodation, though a weaker one, with the other money market targets (total or un-

---

1. Both private expenditure and the demand for money respond positively to income and negatively to interest rates, while net foreign assets respond positively to interest rates and negatively to income. Total reserves are related positively to deposits and negatively to interest rates: borrowing at the central bank rises with the short-term interest rate (central bank lending terms assumed to be constant), while currency is determined by income. For the algebraic formulation of the model, see, Argy, *op. cit.*

borrowed reserves or the monetary base), while the outcome with a DCE target is ambiguous for the same reasons as above. Thus the two targets which got the lowest marks for stabilizing income when the disturbance arises in private expenditures — interest rates and the bank liquidity ratio — have the most desirable properties in insulating the economy from the effects of shifts in the demand for money or between the main components of money.

A *shift* may also occur *in the supply of money* in the form of a change in the demand by banks for reserves. A number of factors, some of them difficult to express in quantitative terms such as anticipations of monetary policy, influence banks' desired reserve levels. Interest rates or DCE would be the targets best designed to insulate economic activity from the undesired impact of unexpected shifts in these levels; in both cases reserve demand would be accommodated. The monetary base and banks' total or unborrowed reserves would be somewhat weaker in their stabilization effects. The most destabilizing target would be the bank liquidity ratio; if the authorities in this case observe a tendency for the ratio to rise, they will withdraw reserves, thus reinforcing the contractionary initial impact. There is accordingly a considerable risk attached to a liquidity ratio policy if banks' demand for reserves is unstable.

It is possible to extend this analysis to mixed cases of shifts in both the demand and supply of money or in either of these, as well as in private expenditures. Such an extension, which would offer concessions to reality since none of the functions surveyed is fully stable, would produce conclusions combining those above and thus offer little guidance in the absence of quantitative specification of the relative importance of the shifts considered. One special and frequent case of a mixed disturbance, however, does warrant further discussion: a shift in a demand component accompanied by a parallel shift in the monetary base. Such a combined shift occurs in an unexpected export boom when the country's international reserves and thereby the monetary base and the money stock tend to run ahead of predictions. It may also occur if fiscal policy has not been properly assessed, say in a situation where the strength of public sector expenditures has been under-estimated, leading to excess demand in the market for goods and excess supply of reserves and money. In such a situation, a monetary base target — involving sterilization of the financial consequences of the external or public sector disturbance — would achieve maximum stabilization. It is conceivable that an external disturbance is purely financial; this is the case when the preferences of non-residents for domestic assets or those of residents for foreign assets change because of a shift in international interest rate differentials or in exchange rate expectations. In such a case, only the adoption of a DCE target will allow the shifts to have an impact on the ultimate objective of achieving a desired income level; each of the other five targets considered here will prompt the authorities to offset the shift and thereby the impact on income.

Despite the restrictiveness of the assumptions on which the above analysis builds — the perusal of only one ultimate objective (income stabilization), the appearance of only one shift or erroneous assessment at a time, and the ability of the authorities to control their chosen target accurately — the conclusions are not without practical applicability. The main consideration in choosing an operating target is the relative degree of predictability in the expenditure, money demand and money supply (i.e. banks' demand for reserves) functions. If the main difficulty is to predict expenditures, the monetary base — and bank credit, if the economy is weakly integrated

141

financially with the rest of the world — is likely to be the most reliable target. If unpredictability is pronounced in the readiness of non-banks to hold financial assets, a target formulated in terms of interest rates is likely to be superior to other targets. Evidence on the past stability of money demand, money supply and expenditure functions in an economy is therefore relevant to the choice of an optimal operating target for monetary policy.

The simplest procedure is to review critically with the help of simulations with an econometric model the accuracy with which these relationships have been accounted for in the past. The most stringent variant of such tests is how well a historical relationship has held up in recent periods when applied to forecasting for, say, several quarters after the end of the sample period for which the relationship was originally estimated. Evidence of this kind is available for most of the six countries; it tends to show that the demand for money is the most stable of these relationships.[1] Unfortunately such a comparison is not fully informative; the results refer to average behaviour in the past and they would not necessarily be a good guide to the relative predictability in a particular situation in which the authorities have to decide on a strategy. For example, there might be evidence of greater past stability in the money demand function and yet reasons to expect that it could shift around substantially over the next 3 to 6 months. An illustration of this type of situation may be found in the United States in 1971. Though the FOMC had at that time swung far towards an aggregate-based strategy, a policy was in fact followed of accommodating short-run shifts in the demand for money, thus minimizing disturbances to income arising out of the money sector. The interpretation of developments in 1971 is still a subject of debate in the United States;[2] there was probably some unintended accommodation in monetary policy as well, but the main point is that the policy followed could be and was at the time rationalized with reference to the prospect of specific instability in the demand for money. Another illustration may be found in the experiences of the United Kingdom during 1971-73, when *Competition and Credit Control* had put more emphasis on the monetary aggregates (pages 81-82). Despite this, a policy was pursued which permitted an unprecedented rapid rate of growth of the aggregates; the rationale was that the demand for bank loans and money had been repressed by rationing and that the banks should be allowed to recapture a larger share of financial markets. It was only at the end of 1973 that quantitative targets were formulated.

As mentioned above, the demand for money function tends on the average, despite the above examples, to be the least unstable of the relationships relevant for choosing a policy target. But the accuracy in predictions after the sample periods is not impressive over short periods, particularly in recent years. For example, a single-equation study of the demand for money in Germany and the United Kingdom completed recently by Hamburger[3] found a root mean square error in predicting the quarter-to-

1. Poole has reviewed some of this evidence for the United States. See *Open Market Policies and Operating Procedures*, Washington D.C. 1971.
2. For a discussion see i.a. Pierce and Thomson in *Controlling the Monetary Aggregates II: The Implementation*, and Hamburger, *Journal of Money, Credit and Banking*, May 1973.
3. M.J. Hamburger, "The Demand for Money in an Open Economy: Germany and the United Kingdom", *unpublished*, April 1974. The demand functions used included nominal income and representative interest rates on substitute financial assets, domestic as well as on Euro-dollar deposits (see pages 93 and 94).

quarter growth (at annual rates) of the narrow money stock (M1) of about 5 percentage points in Germany and 9 percentage points in the United Kingdom during 1971–72. This was admittedly an exceptional period in exchange markets as well as in the two economies; monetary growth was very rapid and inflation accelerated. The ability to predict quarterly movements in money from demand functions is hardly better in Italy. In the three other economies, France, Japan and the United States the shorter-run stability in the income-money nexus appears somewhat greater, though comparable estimates to those reported above are only available for the United States. Using U.S. quarterly data, Goldfeld has found the root mean square error in four quarter predictions to lie in the 2 to 4 percentage points range.[1] Thus it has been somewhat easier in the United States than in either the United Kingdom or Germany to see whether the trend of nominal incomes corresponds to anticipations, though the margin for error remains sufficiently large to cause very difficult problems of interpretation. It cannot be inferred merely from a deceleration (relative to anticipations) of M1 growth by as much as, say, 3 percentage points at an annual rate whether *i*) nominal income has decelerated, *ii*) money demand has shifted downwards, or *iii*) neither of these two events has occurred. In the light of this situation, it is not surprising that the central banks concerned have not rigidly geared the operation of monetary policy to any narrowly prescribed course for any one target. The situation does not, however, warrant a casual attitude towards observed short-run developments in the various possible targets and in other financial variables. On the contrary, there is a need for constant re-evaluation of the main sources of instability in the light of most recent observed developments and prospects.

1. S. Goldfeld, "The Demand for Money Revisited", in A. Okun and G.L. Perry (eds.), *Brookings Papers on Economic Activity*, 1973, Vol.3; the error quoted may be inferred from Table 2, p. 588. It is interesting to note that Goldfeld does not find that there was any important shift in the demand for money in 1971.

BIBLIOGRAPHY

The list of references has been kept to a minimum, since fairly extensive references are given in the five country studies published in the *OECD Monetary Studies Series*. Since no study of United Kingdom monetary policy has been prepared, references to literature on the U.K. experiences are more numerous. A number of investigations have obviously been made of the other five countries since the OECD country studies were completed in 1972-73 and some of the more important ones have also been included in the present bibliography.

1. Amano, A., *International Capital Movements: Theory and Estimation*, Kobe University (unpublished).
2. Andersen, L.C. and Jordan, J.L., "Monetary and Fiscal Actions: A Test of Their Relative Importance", *Federal Reserve Bank of St. Louis Review*, November 1968.
3. Argy, V., "An Evaluation of Financial Targets in Six Countries", *Banca Nazionale del Lavoro Quarterly Review*, March 1974.
4. Artis, M.J. and Lewis, M.K., "The Demand for Money: Stable or Unstable?", *The Banker*, March 1974.
5. Artis, M.J. and Nobay, A.R., "Two Aspects of the Monetary Debate", *National Institute Economic Review*, August 1969.
6. Ball, R.J. and Drake, P.S., "The Impact of Credit Control on Consumer Durable Spending in the United Kingdom, 1957-1961", *The Review of Economic Studies*, October 1963.
7. Bank of England, *Competition and Credit Control*, 1971.
8. Bank of England, *Quarterly Bulletin*.
9. Banque de France, *Bulletin Trimestriel*.
10. Banca d'Italia, *Un Modello Econometrico dell'Economia Italiana (M1, B1)*, Settore Reale e Fiscale, January 1970.
11. Banca d'Italia, *Annual Report*.
12. Bank of Japan, *Economic Statistics*.
13. Bank of Japan, *Monthly Economic Review* (in Japanese).
14. Branson, W.H. and Hill, R.D. Jr., "Capital Movements in the OECD Area", *OECD Economic Outlook, Occasional Studies*, December 1971.
15. Branson, W.H. and Klevorick, A.K., "Money Illusion and the Aggregate Consumption Function", *American Economic Review*, December 1969.
16. Bryant, R.C. and Hendershott, P.H., "Financial Capital Flows in the Balance of Payments of the United States: An Exploratory Empirical Study", *Princeton Studies in International Finance*, No. 25, Princeton University, 1970.
17. Bundesbank, *Monatsberichte*.
18. Bundesminister für Wirtschaft (im Auftrage), *Enquête über die Bauwirtschaft*, Bonn 1973.
19. Burger, A., "Money Stock Control: An Aggregate Approach", *unpublished* (presented at Konstanz Monetary Seminar 1974).
20. Burman, J.P. and White, W.R., "Yield Curves for Gilt-edged Stocks", *Bank of England Quarterly Bulletin*, December 1972.
21. Burman, J.P., "Yield Curves for Gilt-edged stocks: Further Investigation", *ibid.*, September 1973.
22. Caligiuri, G., Fazio, A., Padoa-Schioppa, T., "Demand and Supply of Bank Credit in Italy", *Journal of Money, Credit and Banking*, November 1974.
23. *Consumer Credit*, Report of the Committee, U.K. Secretary of State for Trade and Industry, March 1971.

24. David, J.H., "Un modèle de l'économie française inspiré des thèses monétaristes", *Banque de France, Bulletin Trimestriel*, November 1972.
25. Davis, R.G., "Implementing Open Market Policy with Monetary Aggregate Objectives", *Federal Reserve Bank of New York Monthly Review*, July 1973.
26. Federal Reserve Bank of Boston, *Controlling the Monetary Aggregates I, and II: The Implementation*, Boston 1969 and 1972.
27. *Federal Reserve Bank of St. Louis Review*.
28. *Federal Reserve Bulletin*.
29. Federal Reserve System, Board of Governors, *Open Market Policies and Operating Procedures*, Staff Studies, Washington D.C. 1971.
30. Fisher, G.R. and Sheppard, D., "Some Econometric Analysis on the Impact of Monetary Policy", *OECD Economic Outlook, Occasional Studies*, December 1972.
31. Friedman, B., "Targets, Instruments and Indicators of Monetary Policy", *Harvard Institute of Economic Research Discussion Paper* 347, February 1974.
32. Goldfeld, S.M., "The Demand for Money Revisited", *Brookings Papers on Economic Activity*, 1973:3, Washington D.C., 1973.
33. Goodhart, C.A.E., "The Transmission Mechanism of Monetary Policy", *unpublished* (presented at Konstanz Monetary Seminar 1971).
34. Goodhart, C.A.E. and Gowland, D., "The Relationship between the Yield on Long and Short-dated Gilt-edged Stocks", *unpublished*, 1973.
35. Haache, G., "The Demand for Money in the United Kingdom: Experience since 1971", *Bank of England Quarterly Bulletin*, September 1974.
36. Hamburger, M.J., "The Demand for Money in an Open Economy Germany and the United Kingdom", *unpublished*, 1974.
37. Hamburger, M.J., "Expectations, Long-Term Interest Rates and Monetary Policy in the United Kingdom", *Bank of England Quarterly Bulletin*, September 1971.
38. Hamburger, M.J., "Interest Rates and the Demand for Consumer Durable Goods", *American Economic Review*, December 1967.
39. Hamburger, M.J., "The Lag in Effect of Monetary Policy", *Federal Reserve Bank of New York Monthly Review*, December 1971.
40. Hansen, B., "On the Effects of Fiscal and Monetary Policy: A Taxonomic Discussion", *American Economic Review*, September 1973.
41. Hansen, B., *Fiscal Policy in Seven Countries, 1955–1965*, OECD, Paris 1969.
42. Hardes, H.-D., "Prognosemodel der Wohnungsbauinvestitionen", *Sonderdruck 54*, Institut für Siedlungs-und Wohnungswesen der Westfälischen Wilhelms-Universität, Münster 1971.
43. Hines, A.G.and Catephores, G., "Investment in U.K. Manufacturing Industry 1956–1967", in D. F. Heathfield and K. Hilton (eds.), *The Econometric Study of the U.K.*, 1970.
44. Hodjera, Z., "Short-term Capital Movements of the United Kingdom 1963–1967", *Journal of Political Economy*, July/August 1971.
45. Istituto di Scienze Economiche, "Project LINK, a Quaterly Econometric Model of the Italian Economy", *Discussion Paper* No. 7203, University of Bologna, April 1973.
46. Keran, M.E., "Monetary and Fiscal Influences on Economic Activity: The Foreign Experience", *Federal Reserve Bank of St. Louis Review*, February 1970.
47. Kwack, S.Y., "The Impact of the Smithsonian Exchange Rate Agreement on the U.S. Balance of Payments: An Econometric Analysis", *unpublished*, 1974.
48. König, H., Gaab, W. and Wollens, J., *An Econometric Model for the Financial Sector of the Federal Republic of Germany*, Parts I and II, Discussion Papers 38 and 39, Institut für Volkswirtschaftslehre und Statistik der Universität Mannheim.
49. Modigliani, F., "Monetary Policy and Consumption – the Linkages via Interest Rate and Wealth Effects in the FRB-MIT-Penn Model " in *Consumer Spending and Monetary Policy*, Federal Reserve Bank of Boston 1972.
50. *National Institute Review*, London.
51. Nobay, A.R., "Forecasting Manufacturing Investment – Some Preliminary Results", *National Institute Economic Review*, May 1970.
52. Nullau, B., "Die Wirkungsverzögerungen bei der Finanzierung von Investitionen im Wohnungsbau", *Sonderhefte des Deutschen Instituts für Wirtschaftsforschung*, No. 79, Berlin 1968.
53. OECD Economic Outlook, Nos. 1-14, Paris 1968-1974.
54. OECD Economic Surveys, Paris 1960-1974.

55. OECD *Fiscal Policy for a Balanced Economy*, Paris 1968.
56. OECD Monetary Studies Series, *Monetary Policy in Japan*, Paris 1972.
57. OECD Monetary Studies Series, *Monetary Policy in Germany*, Paris 1973.
58. OECD Monetary Studies Series, *Monetary Policy in Italy*, Paris 1973.
59. OECD Monetary Studies Series, *Monetary Policy in France*, Paris 1974.
60. OECD Monetary Studies Series, *Monetary Policy in the United States*, Paris 1974.
61. OECD, "The Measurement of Domestic Cyclical Fluctuations", *OECD Economic Outlook, Occasional Studies*, July 1973.
62. Porter, M., "Capital Flows as an Offset to Monetary Policy: The German Experience", *IMF Staff Papers*, July 1972.
63. Porter, M. and Kouri, P., "International Capital Flows and Portfolio Equilibrium", *unpublished* (presented at Project LINK annual meeting, Vienna 1972).
64. Rosette, J., "Oekonometrische Investitionsfunktionen für Konjunkturmodelle", *Konjunkturpolitik*, 1971 III.
65. Sitzia, B., "Monetary and Fiscal Influences on Economic Activity: the Italian Experience", *unpublished*, M.I.T., September 1971.
66. Trivedi, P.K., "Inventory Behaviour in U.K. Manufacturing 1956–1967", *Review of Economic Studies*, October 1970.
67. Vicarelli, F., "L'Esportazione di Bancnote nell'Esperienza Italiana dell'Ultimo Decennio", *Studi Economici* 1970.
68. Vipond, M.J., "Fluctuations in Private Housebuilding in Great Britain 1950–1966", *Scottish Journal of Political Economy*, June 1969.
69. Whitehead, C., "A Model of the U.K. Housing Market", *Bulletin of the Oxford University Institute of Economics and Statistics*, November 1971.

OECD PUBLICATIONS, 2, rue André-Pascal, 75775 Paris Cedex 16 - No. 34.171 1975
PRINTED IN FRANCE